PARTNERSHIPS
Machines of possibility

Niels Åkerstrøm Andersen

First published in Great Britain in 2008 by

The Policy Press
University of Bristol
Fourth Floor
Beacon House
Queen's Road
Bristol BS8 1QU
UK

Tel +44 (0)117 331 4054
Fax +44 (0)117 331 4093
e-mail tpp-info@bristol.ac.uk
www.policypress.org.uk

© Niels Åkerstrøm Andersen 2008

British Library Cataloguing in Publication Data
A catalogue record for this book is available from the British Library.

Library of Congress Cataloging-in-Publication Data
A catalog record for this book has been requested.

ISBN 978 1 84742 026 8 (hardback)

Niels Åkerstrøm Andersen is Professor of Political Management at the
Department of Management, Politics and Philosophy, Copenhagen Business
School.

Cover design by Qube Design Associates, Bristol.
Printed and bound in Great Britain by MPG Books, Bodmin.

Contents

List of tables and figures

Tables

Figures

Preface and acknowledgements

Five years ago I began writing a book provisionally entitled *The contractualisation of the universal*. Its aim was to summarise the many different forms of contractualisation that currently take place in the public sector and that all, in a certain sense, frame the concepts of 'general', 'public' and 'common' within the particular form of the contract.

So I created a heuristic distinction between: individual internal contracts between the administration and administration managers or the administration and employees; individual external contracts between the administration and citizens; internal organisational contracts, for example, the so-called internal contracts between departments; and, finally, organisational contracts established outside the administration, for example, between a private company and an administrative department.

Topical forms of contractualisation

	Internal	External
Individual	Management contracts Employee development contracts Supervision contracts	Social contracts Parent contracts Agreement schedules
Organisational	Internal contract management	Outsourcing Partnerships

My efforts, however, quickly became sidetracked, so that the external individual contractualisation, which I had considered a minor issue, eventually evolved into an independent book entitled *The contractualisation of the citizen*, which was published in 2003 (Andersen, 2003a).

Although I am now back on track, once again it has become clear to me that there is more to these contractualisations than I had initially imagined. And once again, a single element of the model (partnerships) has evolved into a book of its own – studying hybrids such as, for example, citizen's contracts or partnerships, came to involve a great number of other issues. Hybrids are phenomena that do not fit into traditional categories and boxes. Deconstruction is typically perceived as a specific research strategy, which seeks out discrepancies and brings impossible relations to light. Hybrids, however, seem to hold in themselves a deconstructive force. They tear at the fundamental building blocks of society, and paradoxes do not impede their efforts. On the contrary, hybrids seem to live off paradoxes. And it is a difficult task to accurately describe this.

This present book is part of a project entitled 'Negotiated Welfare Regime', supported by the Danish Council for Research Policy.

I have received much support during the process of writing this book. I presented a draft for discussion with colleagues at the Department of Management, Politics and Philosophy at the Copenhagen Business School and received many constructive comments. The following people, however, deserve special thanks. Gorm Madsen was the student assistant for the project. Asmund Born read the typescript and has, as always, been an inspiration in making me sharpen, twist and push the analyses to the point where they make a difference. While I was writing the book, Anders la Cour and Holger Højlund worked with very similar questions, and our corridor talks have been important. In 2004, Jeanet Hardis defended her dissertation about multipartite partnerships and I was fortunate enough to be on the assessment committee. Her meticulous empirical studies of partnership management, of the complexity and fragility of partnerships, have worked as a great inspiration for me. Moreover, I would like to thank Klitgaarden for providing a refuge where I could recover my concentration and step on the research pedal. And I wish to especially thank my wife, Hanne Knudsen, who has read through the book draft and has helped me create a much better flow. Thanks to everyone.

Niels Åkerstrøm Andersen
May 2007

Introduction

While 'partnerships' represent one of today's buzzwords, they are more than just a buzzword – for example, they are able to unite the political Right and Left. And endorsing partnerships can also unite the public sector with voluntary organisations, voluntary organisations with private companies, and private companies with the public sector. Buzzwords often become such because they seem to unite a difference or a dilemma, but as a buzzword, 'partnerships' possesses this quality twofold. To the political Centre and the Left, partnerships overcome the dilemma between public shared responsibility and independent social criticism. Partnerships between the public sector and voluntary organisations solve the question of how to unite the systemic independence and critical potential of voluntary organisations with public responsibility for uniting the welfare society. To slightly more conservative groups, partnerships overcome the dilemma between competition and cooperation. Public–private partnerships (PPPs) seem to provide the answer to how to unite the striving towards more competition in the public sector on one hand with cooperation with private companies for the collective benefit on the other hand.

Partnerships are much praised, but often without great accuracy regarding their actual content. Most of us know partnerships as a loose metaphor, which we can inscribe almost any meaning to. We nod our heads and smile at each other in mutual affirmation of the fact that partnerships represent the way forward. But no one sees that we may in fact be speaking from entirely different perspectives and about entirely different concepts, or at least not until the project fails and the partnership does not turn out as desired. This book, therefore, looks at the effort to transform partnerships from a loose metaphor into a binding concept, with the aim of capturing the actual qualities of partnerships. It has subsequently turned into a book covering many concepts – because partnerships are formed in an effort to unite two dilemmas in one form, they involve a multitude of social phenomena.

The concept of partnership as the designation of specific relations between mutually independent organisations is not entirely new. Before the Second World War a partnership indicated a business corporation between single individuals usually composed of close friends or relatives only sometimes supported by a partnership agreement. 'Mutual trust' and 'goodwill' were already buzzwords at that time (Bevis, 1932). In the 1960s and 1970s partnerships were seen as goodwill-driven relations between private companies, particularly in Japanese business (Dore, 1983). These goodwill-driven relations meant that companies failed to take advantage of potential short-term gains in order to maintain long-term relations, for example, from possible lawsuits against business partners in response to contract breaches.

From the mid-1980s we see the articulation of new interorganisational cooperation. The concept of networking became central (Powell and Smith-Doerr, 1994) and it was apparent that networks across different lines of business promoted synergy between different competencies and created innovative cultures. Networking creates innovative advantages without causing smaller companies to lose their flexibility. Particular examples of such interorganisational cooperation were in particular regions in Italy and in particular innovative environments in the US. In Denmark, collaboration between companies became the central focus of many business policies. It led to the establishment of special networking programmes in which banks, consultancies and accountants were trained to work as network brokers, who sought out companies from different lines of business and initiated strategic dialogues between them with the purpose of establishing actual networks (Industriministeriet, 1989; Andersen et al, 1992, pp 126-33).

What distinguishes the concept of partnerships since the mid-1990s is that it is articulated as cross-sectoral cooperation. Today's partnerships not only cut across company boundaries or lines of business; they also cross back and forth between the public, private and voluntary sectors and across policy areas such as, for example, public assistance and public hygiene issues (Ling, 2000; Kurunmäki and Miller, 2004). Or, in other words, partnerships cut across functional systems of communication such as, for example, politics, the economy, education, care and health. This is where the challenge of partnerships lies. Partnerships are designed to be bridges between heterogeneous logics of communication (Jessop, 1999; Anderson-Wallace et al, 2000; Fenwick, 2004; Hardis, 2004).

Partnerships are an international phenomenon. In the United Nations (UN) partnerships are often observed as a form of collaboration that 'can help overcome conflicts, encourage cross-sectoral learning, and turn differences into synergies' (Flyverbom, 2006, p 149). In the UK in particular there has been much discussion of partnerships, not least because of bad experiences with outsourcing. The former Conservative government in the UK introduced PPPs as a way to end the power-dominance of the public sector (Newman, 2001, p 105). The succeeding Labour government has subsequently assumed the partnership rhetoric; however, it sees partnerships as a specific form of regulation, which is capable of overcoming vertical barriers such as state/region/local and horizontal barriers within the public sector between policy areas such as health, education and food policy as well as horizontal barriers between the public, private and voluntary sectors. The UK Department of Health, for example, has developed a partnership programme based on criticism of different boundary conflicts between the areas of social policy and health policy. Here, partnerships offered a solution that made it possible to take on a holistic perspective (Newman, 2001, p 108; Rummery, 2003). In 2000, the UK Department for Education and Skills launched a new programme in relation to lifelong learning that pointed to partnerships between universities, employers and centres for continuing education (CCEs) as the solution in developing new educational degrees, which broke with the hierarchical division, for example, of elementary school, high school and university, and allowed for more flexible paths to higher education, tailored to people's rather differentiated oscillations between work and education through life (Doyle, 2003; see also Fenwick, 2004). In this perspective, companies, CCEs and universities are all perceived as entrepreneurial. The fact that they recognise themselves as such is seen as a basic precondition for the formation of the imagined partnerships. In the words of the Department for Education and Skills: 'The "do nothing" university will not survive' (Doyle, 2003, p 284).

Thus, partnerships are articulated internationally as the solution to various cooperation difficulties across sectoral boundaries. Partnerships are often described in contrast to contracts. They are seen as equivalent to community, long-term cooperation, dialogue, synergy and the utilisation of the mutual differences of the involved parties. Contracts, on the other hand, are seen as equal to opportunistic agreements, short-term calculation and bargaining. However, even though partnerships are defined in almost completely positive terms, they often fail. Social partnerships collapse into indifference or become dissolved in conflicts. PPPs are weighed down by complex organisation and doubt as to whether they will actually prove their worth. Nevertheless, great faith is put in the notion of partnerships today in a number of different areas: PPPs, multipartite partnerships between voluntary, private and public institutions, social partnerships between a company and its employees, partnerships between universities and businesses and, finally, partnerships between western aid organisations and non-governmental organisations (NGOs) in the developing world.

What is the reason that, in many different parts of society, so much energy is poured into an effort to form partnerships? Partnerships can be observed as an attempt to find a functional answer to increasing dependence between societal systems, which at the same time are becoming increasingly different from one another. But partnerships do not simply represent a new concept. In this book it is suggested that we observe partnerships as a new form of contractualisation. It is argued that partnership is a second-order contract, which indicates extensive functional displacements in the organisation of modern society. The differences between contract and partnership are not essential – there are no object-specific differences between contract and partnership. There are, however, extensive differences in the functions of contracts and partnerships respectively – partnerships represent contracts about the development of contracts. As such, they are not only able to handle a large amount of factual complexity but also an enormous temporal complexity. Partnerships are designed to be able to handle the fact that every circumstance of a promise is continually changing. They are designed to maintain the plasticity of the promise, to ensure that contracts remain an on-going creation of contracts and never obtain a fixed form, that what is being fixed is the fact that we are continually in the process of promising each other something, that the place from which the promise is observable as promise can always become displaced. Moreover, partnerships can be seen as a contractual linking of different systems of communication, where the obligation is not primarily in relation to a specific exchange but rather in a project-based obligation towards an imagined future.

This book, therefore, is about the way in which contract as form has come under pressure from increased complexity and demands for constant adaptability.

Five main themes emerge in this book:

- Partnerships represent a functional equivalent to contracts in a hyper-complex society in which the preconditions of more traditional contract forms collapse. Partnerships constitute an answer to the challenge of mutual commitment in a setting where the conditions of a promise are continually changing, where the object of the commitment cannot be clearly defined and where the parties which are to carry the commitment are created and selected along the way.
- Partnerships represent second-order contracts. When you enter into a partnership, you give a promise to subsequently give promises. This has wide-ranging implications for a contract's character of contract, for example, when partnerships as second-order contracts are expected to try to stabilise expectations under the expectation of changing expectations. Most standard contracts can refer to neutral legal grounds by which premises and rules for entering

into a contractual agreement are defined. The grounds on which a partnership functions are only to a certain extent made up of such properties and the partnership has to therefore not only decide the content of the individual partnership but also define its own premises for what defines this partnership as partnership.

- Partnerships allow for new connections between politics, economy, law, health and so on. Partnerships constitute an advanced coupling between a multitude of communication systems that are unable to communicate with one another. Partnerships provide an answer to the increased differentiation of society. They link systems of communication in a way where new possible couplings are continually sought out.

- Partnerships displace the way in which we have negotiated welfare in the welfare state. Welfare negotiations from the mid-1970s on have primarily concerned the allocation of resources to different areas such as hospitals, children and young people, labour market policies and so on. Partnerships between public authorities, private companies and voluntary organisations create multiple individual and delimited negotiation arenas, where what is being negotiated and manipulated is not primarily resources but instead the very definition of welfare responsibilities. Partnerships result in a multiple and particular negotiated welfare regime. This displaces politics from traditional political institutions such as local authorities to the internal negotiations of partnerships.

- Partnerships represent a strange form of order because it is an order that is constantly in the making. One might have a contract but it is not possible to have a partnership since a partnership is essentially partnership formation. A functional contract establishes specific premises for the commitments of the contracting parties and for their subsequent responsibilities. A functional partnership continually produces a surplus of subsequent possibilities for agreements and actions. Partnerships constitute a machine of possibilities on the perimeter of multiple different systems of communication.

In the conclusions to the book the partnership language that has developed is translated into a number of impractical questions. Political institutions, voluntary organisations, private companies and universities are addressed in an effort to point out certain challenges that they ought to take seriously if they truly wish to be serious about entering into partnerships. These questions concern, for example, the fact that private companies have to perceive of and establish themselves as political actors if they are serious about PPPs. And universities have to be careful not to imagine that their business partners understand the concept of knowledge in the same way that they do. To universities, partnerships create a risk of structural corruption of their research. And in their partnerships with the public sector, voluntary organisations have to expect that the public sector may see them as merely another set of institutions to be governed, which is something that could potentially jeopardise the relationship between the voluntary organisation and the voluntary base.

ONE

Analytical strategy

As already indicated, partnerships represent a strange phenomenon; they relate to many different heterogeneous, and often even opposing, expectations. It is therefore not sufficient to interview just a few people who claim to be part of a partnership and to follow them over a period of time. It is also not enough to study a few partnership agreements and to draw conclusions based on them. Or to line up a number of variables and to conduct a partnership survey in order to see which variable responds under which circumstances. When dealing with partnerships, we have to ask: who is the observer? From whose perspective does the partnership emerge and how?

As will be discussed in Chapter Two, partnerships can be comprehended in many different ways. Different actors find partnerships to be meaningful in different ways; a number of metaphors for partnerships even seem to be identical, for example, community, dialogue and trust. As a concept, 'partnership' evens out differences to the point that it becomes hard to know what we are talking about.

A particular approach needs to be employed, therefore, that does not see partnerships as a given phenomenon but rather observes the way in which they are formed and take shape. This approach is referred to as 'observation of the second order'. Without a second-order perspective of observation, the analysis remains too insensitive to the fact that the emergence of partnerships depends on the observer. Without a second-order perspective we run the risk of privileging a random perspective among many actual perspectives on partnerships that might cause us to disregard the fact that the special characteristics of a partnership might be its coupling of many different perspectives. A political scientist sees a network society, a sociologist sees a binding civil society, a lawyer sees the partnership's legal status as agreement, an economist sees a partnership as a strategic alliance and an organisational theorist sees the management and decisions of the partnership. What is interesting is not whether one of them is right, but that they occur at the same time. If we fail to see this, we are unable to describe it, which would mean that the partnership phenomenon had evaded us.

We therefore have to start in a different place in order to capture the concrete social character of a partnership. If not, it becomes too easy to fall back on self-reassuring metaphors, which sidestep the partnership phenomenon in favour of a study of something entirely different, for example, the partnership management, the economy of partnerships or their various legal constitutions. These approaches disregard the partnership as a partnership.

Three epistemological interests

This book comprises three epistemological interests:

- opening up the discussion of partnerships by pointing out its axioms;
- a concretistic interest in the description of the constitution of the operational form of a partnership;
- a diagnostic interest in the description of which societal conditions are at stake as partnerships spread to a growing number of areas.

The first epistemological interest concerns the production of *contingency*. In studying the concrete communicative and discursive creation of the social, the way it could have been created differently is also illustrated. The production of contingency in this context is a question of describing that place of self-evidence from which partnerships are observed in order to provide the discussion and the practice of partnerships with the possibility of seeing their own observations and their axioms. It is a question of providing alternative possibilities for self-description for those who are involved in the creation of partnerships, of holding a mirror to the partnership discourse so that its peculiarities and blind spots become observable.

The second epistemological interest is referred to as *the concretistic epistemological interest*. In brief, the concretistic epistemological interest is about observing the social as it appears concretely, and it is a question of seeing the social as it is concretely created in communicative or discursive operations. Foucault calls discourse analysis 'pure description of the facts of discourse' (Foucault, 1998, p 306). He even maintains that the spirit of discourse analysis is a 'felicitous positivism' (Foucault, 1972, p 234). Elsewhere he writes: 'Each moment of discourse must be welcomed in its irruption as an event.... There is no need to retrace the discourse to the remote presence of its origin; it must be treated in the play of its immediacy' (Foucault, 1998, p 306). The questions in this context are: in which communicative operations do partnerships emerge and how? What is the communicative form of operation that establishes partnerships as partnerships? Much literature about partnerships presuppose that we know what a partnership is. Or we are provided with a short definition, which then forms the basis for studies of empirical variants and the dissemination of partnerships. However, this creates a strange condition in research where empirical knowledge about a partnership accumulates without the generation of insight into the partnership's concrete character of social phenomenon. What is interesting is the way in which partnerships obtain the concrete character of a partnership. This chapter looks at the concrete operational modus of partnerships, which results in a paradox, that is, that this requires a fair amount of abstract conceptual work.

The final epistemological interest is referred to as the *diagnostic epistemological interest*. This is about diagnosing the space of possibility of communicative practice. It is a question of inquiring into current conditions of possibility, not in order to understand our age, not in order to explain our age, not in order to predict or define it, but simply to map out the positively possible. It is about seeing how partnerships open up spaces of action and possibility. What changes do partnerships instigate in what is communicatively possible? What is topically and socially put at stake through partnerships? This interest does not constitute fact-based insight into the specific premises for someone's prospective decision to enter into a partnership. It represents insight into openings, an insight whose character of insight ultimately depends on whether the actors whom the analyses concern experience the diagnosis as 'apposite' or as 'missing the point'. Or, in other words, to the extent that the three above-mentioned epistemological interests can be said to subscribe to the notion of critical research, it is not up to the research itself to determine whether or not it is critical. Criticism is always, and cannot be anything but, self-criticism, and hence the research recipients are sovereign in providing or not providing the research with its critical qualities.

The three epistemological interests can without doubt be pursued through different analytical strategies with roots in, for example, Michel Foucault, Reinhardt Koselleck and so on. In this book, they are pursued by means of Niklas Luhmann's systems theory (Luhmann, 1993c). However, in harnessing Luhmann's systems theory to the three epistemological interests, something happens to it. At present there exist different approaches to Luhmann's systems theory. The predominant approach in Germany is referred to as scholastic systems theory. This approach conceives of systems theory as a closed but incomplete work. The closure came with Luhmann's death and since then it has constituted a new canon to sociologists, which has to be maintained and interpreted. In this tradition, one can work scholastically within the theoretical framework, point out smaller or bigger theoretical problems, provide suggestions for improvements or compare functionally equivalent solutions to these theoretical problems. Another understanding of systems theory emphasises the explanatory force in Luhmann's social theory. This pertains in particular to the Anglo-Saxon way of employing systems theory. It is based on the conviction that, comparatively speaking, Luhmann's theory about the functional differentiation of society is superior in representing the complexity of society. This approach has a higher degree of empirical openness; however, empirical typically refers to something that has to be explained within Luhmann's diagnosis of the functionally differentiated society. This becomes a strange Parsonian reading of Luhmann, in which systems theory is seen as a net of theoretical hypotheses. It is then possible to choose a career as the Luhmann representative within a given field – the Luhmann representative in jurisprudence, in international politics, in organisational theory, and so on. A third way is referred to as the path of analytical strategy (Andersen, 2003c; see also Gibson et al, 2005; Klemm and Glasze, 2005). Urs Stäheli refers to it as deconstructive systems theory (Stäheli, 2000). The objective here is not to produce a new interpretation of a given phenomenon, in this case a systems theory interpretation. It is a question of defining Luhmann's epistemological notion of second-order observation as the only fixed basis. The central effort, then, becomes the unfolding of the three above-mentioned epistemological interests through the observation of actual observations as observations. Thus perceived, systems theory becomes an empirical science, albeit of a specific kind, related to post-structuralist empirical sciences such as discourse analysis and deconstruction. The central effort does not become theory development; rather it opens up the actual empirical sociality through deconstructive systems theory observation, and in this, Luhmann's many theories, and among them his theory of functional differentiation, constitute not something to be represented but instead something to read up against, something that also has to be deconstructed, twisted, displaced in the analytical strategic effort. Systems theory represents a form of interest in practice, a way of posing impractical questions to practice.

Observation of the second order

As mentioned, these three epistemological interests are pursued by means of what Luhmann refers to as 'observation of the second order'. Thus, at the heart of this book lies a very specific epistemology and a very specific concept of observation, which embraces a programme about the observation of observations as observations.

Luhmann defines observation as an indication within the framework of a difference. All observations operate by means of a difference. When an observation fastens onto something in the world, a distinction is drawn between this 'something' and everything else. What the observer sees only becomes indicated and visible through the observation's relationship to that which it is distinguished from. This means that it is the difference that comes to indicate how observation takes place. A partnership, for example, is not simply a partnership. It is always a partnership to an observer, which means that the way the partnership is a partnership depends on the difference through which observation takes place. The way in which a partnership becomes visible in an observation with the difference between regulator/regulated is different, for example, from observations with the difference between pay/not pay. In the former observation, the partnership becomes a regulatory form whose capacity for regulation is comparable to other forms of regulation, for example, hierarchy or law. And the observer emerges as someone whose intentions with the partnership relate to regulatory issues. In the latter observation, partnerships become observable as a business transaction among other possible business transactions. Does it or does it not pay off to enter into this partnership? What is in it for us? And the observer, as a result, becomes a homo economicus with an eye for scanty resources and their distribution.

The point is that every observation is an operation, drawing a distinction that at the same time remains invisible to the observation itself. The observation always indicates one side of this distinction and leaves the other side unmarked, although it still guides the observation. A partnership is seen as a flexible regulatory form but the perspective and the distinction that gives the partnership these particular qualities is not seen. The division of the world into govern/governed is not seen, only the fact that partnerships are about governing. In other words, an observation sees what it sees but does not see that it does not see what it does not see. An observation cannot see the distinction with which it observes. The distinction defines the blind spot of the observation. And this book therefore concerns those differences through which partnerships operate and their many blind spots.

With reference to Spencer-Brown, Luhmann refers to the inside of the difference as the indicated side (m) and the outside of the difference as the non-indicated side (Spencer-Brown, 1969; see also Robertson, 1999). The blind spot constitutes the very unity of the difference, which both separates the two sides and holds them together in one difference. This is called the calculus of form and is formalised below in Figure 1.1.

Figure 1.1: Calculus of form

Form

An observation indicating something in the world cannot simultaneously indicate itself. However, a new observation is able to observe the observation. Such an observation can observe both the fact that indication takes place and the difference within which indication takes place. It can observe the blind spot of the first observation. This is the epistemological programme of Luhmann's systems theory: to observe the blind spots of other observations, the second order (Luhmann, 1988b, 1990a, 1993b).

Second-order observation is to observe observations as observations. This concentrated statement, 'to observe observations as observations', comprises at least three central points.

The first point is that observations cannot be observed as the expression of anything outside the observation itself, for example, conservative or liberal ideologies, economic structures, crises or invisible manipulating intentions. From a second-order perspective, an observation is not seen as the wilful intention of an observer. This would displace the focus on the observation itself onto a psychological or sociological interpretation of the observer. It does not make sense to conduct an analysis of the observer's wilful intentions – we cannot simultaneously observe the observation as observation and also see observation as the expression of will. In a second-order perspective, the observer is seen rather as a parasite on the observation. It is the observation that observes and the observation's operation of drawing distinctions defines the way in which the observer comes into view. In a second-order perspective, the observation is also not seen as expressing a structural definition of observation. The individual subject is not being replaced with a structural subject, where it is the economic structure, linguistic structure or ideological structure that speaks and observes. And it is not being claimed that such analyses are wrong, but it is not possible to observe observations in their independent positivity and simultaneously see them as the expression of something else. The world does not ask to be observed in a particular way. The world is what it is. But what is of interest is the way the world comes into view and how this affects the way we interact with it.

The second point is that the above is only possible to the extent that observations are seen as independent operations. An observation is an operation, and as such it consists of pure topicality. It exists in its operation or it does not exist at all.

The third point also pertains to the observation of the object. You are what you say. Second-order observation is at the same time first-order observation and takes place therefore within the framework of a distinction. Thus, it is not a privileged position of observation above other observations. The conditions pertaining to the first order also pertain to the second order. The theory of observation encompasses itself, so to speak. The difference with which second-order observations observe is the distinction between indication/difference. Thus, we can formalise an observation as the unity of the difference (see Figure 1.2).

Figure 1.2: The form of observation

Indication | Difference

Observation

This means that second-order observations are highly reductionistic – they see only indications and differences and nothing else, which is the necessary price for this strategy of deactivation of axioms. It also implies a basic renunciation of the answer to questions of why and questions of what.

So, observations should be observed as such in their momentary scarcity and not as something else, and this is precisely what gives systems theory its strength in deactivating axioms. It is a form of neo-concretism – it represents an insistence on staying with the observations rather than immediately shifting the focus away from them onto their context of causes or meaning. Observations are not to be interpreted or explained. They are merely to be described and diagnosed: which distinction is used in the observation? How is the blind spot defined? How can new observations be added? This is also how the 'gibbet' (⌐) is used. It forces me to stay with the simple distinction, to maintain and observe it.

Society as communication

The focus here is on communicated observations of partnerships or partnerships as communication. The central issue is partnerships as social and communicative phenomena, which brings us to the second fundamental point of departure for this book – society consists of communication and only communication. Therefore the fundamental event of the social is considered to be communication rather than action.

Communication is not a particular form of action in which a sender sends a message to a recipient and in which communication is seen as successful once the recipient has understood the message as the sender intended it. By contrast, in systems theory communication is defined as a network of retrospective connections (Luhmann, 1996). When something is said, a horizon and capacity of connection is formed. This is called 'connectivity', for example, someone makes a sarcastic comment about something to a colleague. The remark opens up many subsequent connections from the colleague, which may take the communication in a number of different directions. Perhaps there is no answer, that is, no connections to the horizon of connectivity, which means that no communication is developed. Perhaps the colleague connects with the communication from the premise that they are affected by the sarcasm; perhaps they connect through a literal interpretation of the sarcasm or perhaps they respond with a joke. The point is that it is impossible to determine whether or not communication will take place until the connection of the next communication, and, just as importantly, the next communication determines the communication's character as, for example, serious, literal or witty. Thus, communication is essentially different from speech acts. In this perspective, communication consists of selection, where a connection produces new connectivity, and so on. Communication has its own life, which no individual participant is able to control. Consider, for example, a meeting: a manager may have made meticulous plans for the proceedings of a meeting, and yet the agenda slips. Themes are opened up that were not meant to be and themes that were meant to be dealt with only briefly turn out to open up more connectivities than desired. Seemingly, the planned decisions were made, but at the next meeting in which the minutes are approved, it turns out that what seemed a clear decision is later agreed on merely as a discussion.

Communication has a life of its own, and this is the material of society. In this context partnerships are observed as communication and the question is the way in which partnerships are constituted communicatively. Hence, different players and their reasons for entering into partnerships will not be studied; rather, the focus will be on the formation of communicative expectation in the context of partnerships. In what way do we communicate about partnerships? Do partnerships link different systems of communication, each with their own perspective on partnerships? Do partnerships represent a particular form of communication with their own inherent logic of expectation formation?

In social systems, operations of observation and system formation take place through communication. Social systems consist of communication and nothing but communication. Communication constitutes three operations: of information selection (what is the information going to be about?), selection of the form of message (how to inform?) and selection of understanding (how is the message to be understood?). Without all three elements, there is no communication. However, we should not perceive understanding of communication in a psychological sense. Understanding does not mean the way in which a system of consciousness takes in the message. Rather, it simply means the way in which the next communication connects and chooses one possibility in a horizon of connectivity. Any message opens up for a multitude of possible connections. A message might be perceived as humorous, literal, inviting, dictating, and so on. There is always a surplus of possible connections. In terms of systems theory, understanding is defined as the selection of connection in relation to possibilities for connections defined as connectivity. Only when there is connection is there communication.

Thus, communication is created retrospectively or recursively. It is always the next communication that determines whether communication takes place and how. Every connection opens up for a horizon of possibilities for new connections (connectivity) and becomes communication only once a new connection makes a selection among these. This also means that no one is able to control the communication. No single communication participant is able to decide the continued communication. In this sense, the communication has 'a life of its own'. Social systems represent, in other words, autopoietical systems, creating themselves on the basis of communication as a network of recursive operations (Luhmann, 1995b; for a critique of Luhmann's concept of autopoiesis, see Münch, 1992).

In other words, social systems can be perceived as a net of recursive communication, which employs operations of distinction to create, stabilise or displace expectations to the continuation of the communication (Luhmann, 1990b, 1995a). The fact that someone not only thinks but also articulates 'She is sweet' creates expectations as to the communication's continuation. The recipient expects the sender to expect the recipient to either confirm or deny the statement that she is sweet. It is not expected, for example, of the recipient to utter, 'Have you heard tomorrow's weather report?'. However, the recipient can never be sure of the sender's expectations. Only the indicated side is visible and potentially speaking, 'sweet' may represent the actualisation of a number of differences, for example, sweet/unkind, sweet/sour, sweet/unappealing, sweet/smart. Once the difference between sweet/sour has been confirmed, the difference stabilises the expectations between the communication participants for the continuation of the communication. Thus, the difference maps out not only individual observations but also communicative observations, perceived as expectations related to the continuation of the communication. Differences create possibilities for connections and horizons of connectivity within which the communication can move.

A social system consists of pure topicality, of communicative operations, which continually disappear and which only create momentary retrospective connections to other operations. Each individual communicative operation either confirms and condenses previous communication or displaces the movement of formation and enables the emergence of a new system of communication with new expectations for the continuation of the communication (Clam, 2000). Thus a communicative input can either (1) be *confirmed*, which means that the communication is continued on the marked side of the communicative guiding difference, (2) be *contradicted*, which means that the difference is traversed and the communication continues in the same form but on the unmarked side, (3) be *displaced*, which means that a new difference is introduced with a new horizon of connectivity, or (4) be *terminated*, which means that no connection takes place and no new horizon of expectations is established. Thus, ⌐ is not only a difference for the way in which something is observed, it is also a difference that creates an expectation for the possible continuation of the communication.

In effect, autopoietical systems are operatively closed. This closure lies in the very split mechanism of the operations; the fact that the differences have two sides that means that subsequent operations can only connect with either one or the other side or change form by means of a new distinction, which again only means the creation of a new system. The economic system of communication, for example, operates within the form of payment or non-payment, and the continuation of economic communication depends therefore on an act of payment or non–payment. Economic communication cannot be continued by means of an expression of love. This would not be a recursive connection but a displacement of the form and hence the potential of a different system of communication.

In stressing the fact that communication has a life of its own, which no individual communication participant is able to control, the analytical fruitfulness of maintaining a very clear distinction between systems of communication and systems of consciousness is argued. Systems of consciousness are able to participate in communication but they are unable to communicate with one another. Systems of consciousness cannot recursively link up with each other's operations – that would constitute mind-reading. On the contrary, we might say that communication is only possible precisely because systems of consciousness are unable to connect to each other's operations. There is a difference between what a system of consciousness articulates and what it thinks. If both were visible, communication would quickly break down. Individual people do not always speak their true opinions about someone else. It is one thing to think that the other person is an idiot; it is something else to say it. If both the actually spoken and the thought were available for the connection of the other person, there would be a breakdown in communication. A system of consciousness can link up with communication, but communication can only link up with other communication – only communication can communicate. Systems of consciousness are destined to function as the environment of communication. In terms of analytical strategy, operations of observation are to be observed precisely as observations. It is a question of remaining concrete in relation to communication as operations and not to become tempted to shift the focus onto the communication participants, but to observe the communication as communication without reducing it to individual motives and intentions, which are invisible in the communication and which the observer can only guess about. Hence the importance of the clear distinction. The difference between communication as an act and social systems as a flow and net of recursive operations of communication can be summarised as shown in Figure 1.3:

Figure 1.3: Communication in systems theory as opposed to action theory

Communication as recursive net of operations

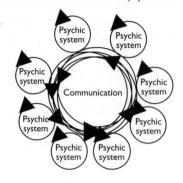

Communication can be neither a success nor a failure; it can only continue, become displaced or discontinue

Communication as action

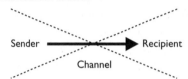

Inherent notion of successful communication when the reception is equal to the sending

Four analytical strategies for second-order observation

There is a wealth of possibilities for second-order observation (Andersen, 2003c). Generally speaking, second-order observation presupposes guiding differences for the establishment of a second-order perspective. A guiding difference creates the second-order perspective by dividing the world into second-order observation and the observed observations. However, not all differences can function as guiding differences for second-order observation. Only differences that can appear as a part of its own whole are able to function as guiding differences. The reason for this is that a second-order perspective has to be able to include itself. An observation of the second order has to be able to embrace itself as an observation in order not to become what Foucault referred to as 'discourse commentary', that is, an observation from a level different than the object. Observations observed by a second-order observer are of the same nature as the observations of them. In effect, only concepts, which can appear as part of their own whole, can constitute the perspective for an observation of the second order.

This means that differences employed to guide second-order observation *have to* be traceable as first-order differences. If we observe through the distinction between man/woman and cannot trace this difference as an active operative difference in the material, then the observation is not of the second order but only of the first. Second-order observation only becomes second order through its capacity as a repetition of the first order. If you insist on observing by means of the distinction between man/woman where it is not actively employed as a distinction operation in the observed communication, then you comment on the communication from a different place. You do not observe the observations as observations in their concrete momentary scarcity (see also Luhmann, 1988a). A frequently employed guiding difference in systems theory is the difference between system/environment. When second-order observing with this difference, you observe precisely the way in which the communication *itself* makes distinctions between itself and its environment. You observe the way in which the communication emerges as a system in the communication and the way that it observes with the communication something that the communication is precisely not. Thus, second-order communication constitutes a specific doubling of the object.

Second-order observation presupposes, therefore, second-order concepts. In order to be able to observe observations as observations we have to observe by means of concepts capable of conceptualising themselves. They have to be autological (Esposito, 1996; Robert, 1997). This is the minimum requirement for second-order observation and it defines, therefore, a boundary for which differences can function in terms of analytical strategy.

One example of a second-order concept, which will be elaborated on below, is Kosseleck's concept of concept. Here, a concept is defined as the unity of the difference between concept/counterconcept, and with this definition, the concept is able to describe itself. One example of a concept that does not pass this test is the concept of interest. Observing different communication participants as interested parties in an attempt to uncover the interests underlying their statements and actions divides the world into players with specific interests. However, if we employ this perspective to observe the perspective itself, we run into difficulties. We are forced to ask a question that we are unable to answer: what interest motivates the interest analysis' ascription of specific interest to specific players? Another example of a difference that does not pass the test could be between elite/people. A lot of democracy research employs this distinction, but again: does this form of democracy analysis express the voice of the elite or that of the people? Is the distinction itself elitist or popular? It is not being suggested that such differences cannot generally be employed in research, but to the extent that your aspirations go in the direction of some form of discourse or systems analytics, they cannot be used.

This 'testing' of differences primarily has a negative function. It can justify the exclusion of differences that lack the capacity to function as guiding differences. Differences without the capacity to appear as a part of their own whole cannot be used in observation of the second order. The testing does not, however, provide positive justification for the selection of differences: why this particular guiding difference and not another?

The only response to this is to say that this weakness precisely represents the strength of systems theory. It installs the possibility of playing with guiding differences. In systems theory, pointing out that the chosen guiding difference cannot be substantiated but has to simply begin is never the mere expression of politeness or empty invocation. The question 'Why this particular guiding difference?' opens up for other guiding differences and is an inherent element of the analytical-strategic machine about continuing to play with the guiding differences in order to see the way in which the observed observations emerge. What is unique about Luhmann's systems theory is the degree to which it opens up while, at the same time, creating the possibility of actually controlling and re-closing. The question, 'Why this particular guiding difference?' opens up in a radical way for the choice of new guiding differences. Thus, to a great extent, carrying out a systems-theoretical analysis becomes a question of playing with guiding differences. Long before you start to write seriously, the work is about developing and testing guiding differences in relation to the empirical material (the observations that are to be observed) in order to see which interesting and intriguing observation might emerge. Systems theory is not a bookkeeper's science concerned with mapping out and categorisation. It is not a science in the name of death and order but of life and multiplicity. Systems theory must not only derive from a sense of uneasiness in relation to the world but has to also generate a sense of discomfort in 'the reading systems' in the form of doubting the given and familiar. It is not simply a question of seeing something new, something else or something more. It is a question of challenging practice in its way of seeing, of offering practice the chance to see anew. Ultimately, it is a question of acting on the three introduced epistemological interests: the production of contingency, concretism and diagnostics.

Each analytical strategy is therefore based in guiding the way in which observations are observed as observations. In this book, four guiding differences are primarily employed and hence a combination of four different analytical strategies: the semantic analysis, the form analysis, the formation analysis and the coupling analysis. These are described briefly and somewhat simplified as follows. The guiding difference of *the semantic analysis* is between concept/meaning (Luhmann, 1993f). Semantic analysis is employed to study how meaning and expectations become condensed into concepts and form semantic reservoirs that are available to communication.

A concept consists of a condensation and generalisation of a multiplicity of meaning and expectations. A concept *condenses* expectations by reducing many heterogeneous expectations into concepts. Concepts are never unambiguously definable. If we are told about someone that he is an accountant, we immediately refer to a horizon of different expectations, for example, 'he is a bookkeeper type', 'he is a control freak', 'he thinks in boxes', 'he has integrity', and so on. Thus, a concept represents a form of expectational structure. Using a specific concept in communication establishes expectations about expectations of the communication and its continuation. Moreover, concepts are *general* since a concept is never identical to its particular use in a particular communication. The concept is generally available to communication but obtains in the communication a specific meaning and creates specific expectations.

The concept of 'state', for example, links together a multiplicity of meaning elements such as, for example, taxation, territory, legal exercise of power, bureaucracy and citizenry. The concept 'voluntary organisation' links together entirely different meaning elements, for example, independence, dissidence, civil society, popular, non-bureaucratic, informal, driven by commitment. The multiplicity of meaning always becomes fixed in the form of a concept by the difference between concept and counterconcept as illustrated in Figure 1.4.

Figure 1.4: The concept of concept

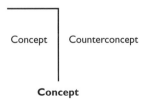

There is no concept without a counterconcept to keep the concept in place (Koselleck, 1985; Luhmann, 1993d, p 15). The counterconcept defines restriction for the concept. A conceptual pair could be man/woman, where the meaning condensed into the concept of woman sets the restrictions for the meaning of 'man'. The expectations associated with being a woman define the restrictions for what can be expected of someone who is indicated in the communication as manly (with or without penis). Another example could be partnership/contract where a partnership would be defined precisely as a non-contract and everything that we associate with a contract, for example, formal, short term, inflexible and controlling. A third example could be the concept of 'social worker', which is precisely only a social worker in relation to a client, and what is expected of a social worker is therefore entirely dependent on which expectations relate to 'client' as its counterconcept. The struggle over the social worker is about the description of the client and the expectations condensed into the concept of client, for example, self-reliant, active and independent or despondent, helpless and struggling.

In relation to this, semantics designates the reservoir of concepts available to systems of communication. In the semantic analysis we are able to distinguish between three meaning dimensions, which point out certain 'arch-differences' to the semantic analysis. The *social dimension* is the dimension for the semantic construction of social identities by which there exists only one 'us' (concept) in relation to a 'them' (counterconcept). 'Us' is only us in relation to and as different from 'them', but 'they' only exist as they in 'our' reference to 'them'. This means that expectations of 'others' create the boundary for expectations of 'ourselves'. The *factual dimension* is the dimension for the semantic construction of factual relations in which 'things' are ordered in relation to one another and in relation to 'us'. And finally, the *time dimension* is the dimension for the construction of 'us-in-time', where the present is always suspended between future (concept) and past (counterconcept). The future represents a horizon of expectations and the past a space of experience, and the present is always only in the tension between these two. The three dimensions can be formalised as shown in Figure 1.5.

Semantic analysis asks: how are meaning and expectations formed and how do these become condensed and generalised in concepts that together establish certain semantic reservoirs for systems of communication? This includes the question of how concepts are displaced so that they might be given new counterconcepts or how counterconcepts become counterconcepts to new concepts or how a

Figure 1.5: The three meaning dimensions

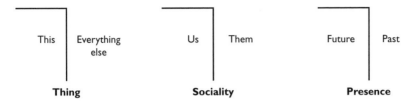

This	Everything else		Us	Them		Future	Past
Thing			**Sociality**			**Presence**	

counterconcept becomes non-specific so a struggle ensues with respect to giving it meaning.

An analysis based on systems theory typically begins with a semantic analysis. As we cannot know in advance the way in which a particular question or phenomenon presents itself, we may begin by studying the origin of the semantic, which sheds light on the historical and possibly spatial variability of the question.

The guiding difference of the *form analysis* is unity/difference (Luhmann, 1999). Form analysis observes the unity of the differentiation formation of an observational operation. It is aimed at fundamental forms of communication. While there are endless amounts of differences available to communication, a small but indefinite number of these differences establish forms of communication that other differences link up with. Some of these are forms of decision, transaction, intimacy and care. These forms of communication each have their communicative logic, their mutually exclusive way of constantly splitting up communication into marked and unmarked. The focus here is on whether and how partnerships can also be perceived as a fundamental form of communication. The questions in form analysis are: what is the difference within which operations take place? Which form is held together in a unity? These questions include certain sub-questions. When indicating X, what is the other side of the difference? That is, what is located on either side of the difference? What is the tension between the two sides? How can communication continue to operate through the same distinction? How is the blind spot of the difference defined? How does it establish the conditions of impossibility for the continuation of the communication? Which observer emerges when the observer operates through the difference? In general, how is the *form* of communication established through which a system can create and unfold itself and which becomes repeated in all of the system's operations, elements and differentiations?

Any form establishes a paradox. It divides what cannot naturally be divided. The relation between the inside and outside of the form is always a relation of impossibility so the objective of a form analysis is to specify the specific conditions of impossibility for the forms of communication from which the communication is forced to create possibilities. It is a question of the interminable inner logic of the forms of communication and operation.

In other words, form analysis studies the fundamental differences through which communication operates and which causes any communication within the form to be placed on either the inside or outside of the form. The form determines expectations with respect to the continuation of the communication. However, precisely because expectations are always tied to a difference, there will always be a point where the expectations break down. Within law, communication takes place within the form right/wrong. But the difference can collide with itself if the communication inquires into its own form within the system of expectations of the form itself, for example, is the law itself right or wrong? This cannot be determined, and this is the fundamental paradox of legal communication, its condition of impossibility, the inner logic that all legal communication is forced to unfold. The purpose of the form analysis is to display this inner logic of specific kinds of communication. It is a question of the boundary of expectation formation given a particular dividing operation in the communication.

The guiding difference of the *formation analysis* is form/medium (Luhmann, 1997). A form merely constitutes a unity or a fixed coupling in relation to the loose elements it links together. Media, in turn, are loosely coupled elements whose quantity is always such that they can never be absorbed or configured by a form. However, as loosely coupled elements, media are only loose in relation to forms. Moreover, media are only observable when imprinted in a form. Money represents an example of a medium of communication that becomes visible as a medium precisely when it is imprinted in the form of decision. When an organisation decides to invest its money in a particular stock portfolio, the medium of money becomes imprinted in decision as form. The characteristic of money as a medium lies precisely in the fact that it might be formed in a wide range of different communications other than the specific decision to invest. It could have been formed in a discussion about the prioritisation of social responsibility and hence be tied to an entirely different meaning. Once the investment has been made, the link to the investment decision is suspended and the money circulates in entirely different communications. The 'concrete investment decision' as form, however, cannot be recirculated in the same way. Two coins or notes can be exchanged as a matter of course. Two concrete decisions cannot.

Luhmann distinguishes between three kinds of media (a distinction that is not exhaustive): *language, media of dissemination* such as, for example, newspapers and television and *symbolically generalised media* such as, for example, money and power. In fact, the difference between form/medium allows for two different analytical strategies depending on which side of the difference is defined as the indicated side. Thus, we can speak of a medium analysis when emphasising the side of medium: medium/form. And we speak of formation analysis when emphasising the side of form: form/medium.

Medium analysis inquires into the formation of media and into the way in which media establish possibilities for certain forms of communication. For example, how has money become established as a symbolically generalised medium and which new forms of communication might money give rise to? That is, how and within which forms can communication take place when the medium is money? In medium analysis, an organisation becomes observable as a potential medium, that is, a possible way to form decisions.

Formation analysis focuses on what happens to the form when different media become imprinted into it. How do using different media affect the form in different ways? In this book, the form is most often an organisation communicating through decisions. In every communicative operation in an organisation the form of decision is used continually, dividing the world into fixed and open contingency in relation to social expectations. However, decisions only operate in the formation of a symbolically generalised medium, for example, money, power, passion, works, 'the unformed child' and law (Andersen, 2003b). These symbolically generalised media have not been generated within the autopoiesis of the organisations but by the function systems of society such as the economic system, the political system, the system of love, the system of art, the educational system and the legal system. A formation analysis asks: when and how are which media formed in an organisation and with which effects for the possible continuation of the organisational communication? From such a perspective, the organisation can be observed as a form that deflects different media in flows of decisions.

Finally, the guiding difference of the *coupling analysis* is coupling/differentiation. It is about specifying the way in which systems let themselves be disturbed by each other even though they are operatively closed in relation to each other. Systems theory becomes exceedingly sensitive to systems relations because they are not seen as self-evident. Because systems are considered operatively closed, the analysis becomes sensitive to the 'mechanisms' that in spite of the closed nature of the systems create their openness and mutual couplings. When communication between systems is not self-evident, the analysis develops a keen eye for the character of systems relations. Thus, the coupling analysis asks: how are systems linked at the same time as their differentiation is maintained?

Luhmann points out that systems of communication are autopoietical systems that create all the elements of which they consist. A system cannot create elements for another system; they can merely produce their own internal order. Systems of communication are operatively closed in that their operations link up with each other recursively. On the other hand, they are cognitively open through observation. Systems can observe their environment, including other systems, but they cannot operate in the environment or in other systems. And systems cannot communicate with each other. The ways in which they draw their boundaries of meaning are fundamentally different, that is, they form meaning in different ways. They can observe each other's communication and they can also ascribe meaning to each other's communication, but based solely on their own forms of communication. Teubner refers to this as the system's ability to generate productive misconceptions of another system's communication (Teubner, 1991). One example could be the legal system's communication of a number of new rulings in which the discharge of company waste is found to be illegal and fines are issued. The economic system can of course observe this but only in terms of economy. The legal communication becomes productively (mis)conceived as a price setter of waste discharge.

The fact that systems cannot communicate with each other but can in turn observe each other enables structural couplings between them. Structural couplings represent forms of simultaneous operations. They can provide the systems with a continual flow of disorder in response to which the systems are able to create and change themselves.

Couplings are always only couplings in relation to mutually closed systems. Structural couplings presuppose systems differentiation. However, this difference between coupling and differentiation also has to be part of the form of the coupling itself since a coupling cannot exist in the space between systems. A coupling has to be in the individual system and from that place both connect and separate the systems. We might say that every coupling in itself has to represent a unity of the re-entry of the difference between coupling/differentiation. A structural coupling between systems of communication can simply be defined as the unity of irritation from other systems and indifference to other systems (Luhmann, 1992b, p 1433).Therefore, coupling analysis has to specify the way in which a coupling opens up for a particular form of irritation of a communication system within the system itself and the way in which the coupling at the same time ensures indifference so that the system does not become overpowered by irritation. The general form of structural coupling is shown in Figure 1.6.

Figure 1.6: Structural coupling

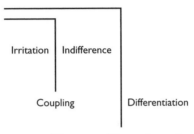

The general form of coupling

Conclusion

The four analyses are summarised below in Table 1.1. Using partnership as an example, the right hand column illustrates the way in which observation is observed differently depending on the guiding difference.

Semantic analysis observes the way in which a partnership is observed through different concepts.Thus, partnership emerges as a concept and the question becomes the way in which meaning and expectations become condensed over time into the concept of partnership and

Table 1.1:The four analytical strategies

Analytical strategy	Guiding difference	Partnership observed as...
Semantic analysis	Concept/meaning	Semantic domain of internal linguistic horizon of expectation
Form analysis	Unity/difference	Reproduction of fundamental unity and operational form
Formation analysis	Form/medium	The linking of communication operations in flows of formations
Coupling analysis	Coupling/differentiation	Organised sensitivity/insensitivity

with which counterconcepts and expectations in relation to contracts. It is a question of the semantic preconditions for observing and communicating about partnerships including the linking of specific communicative expectations in relation to partnerships. This is shown in Figure 1.7.

Figure 1.7: Partnership as concept

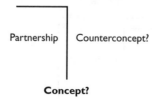

In form analysis it is a question not of observing the way in which partnerships are observed but how observation and communication can take place *by means of* a partnership as a specific form of communication. That is, what does the world look like through the glasses of partnership? This is shown in Figure 1.8.

Figure 1.8: Partnership as form

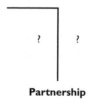

Formation analysis observes the way in which different media such as law, power and money are moulded into a partnership as form or similar forms, for example, outsourcing. A partnership then emerges as an organisation that develops media and is coloured by the media it develops. It is a question of the mutual deflection and interference in the form of the different media (see Figure 1.9).

Finally, coupling analysis is about whether and how contracts have the capacity to link different systems together and hence create simultaneity of operations in different systems of communication (see Figure 1.10).

Figure 1.9: Partnership forms media

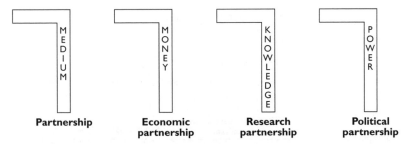

| Partnership | Economic partnership | Research partnership | Political partnership |

Figure 1.10: Partnership as structural coupling

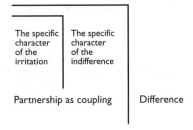

With these analytical strategies in mind, we are now able to present the partnership question anew. The strategy slowly expands on the question by continuously displacing the second-order perspective so that something new emerges, either by observing through a different guiding difference or by slightly displacing the point of observation (see Figure 1.11 overleaf).

Figure 1.11: Question

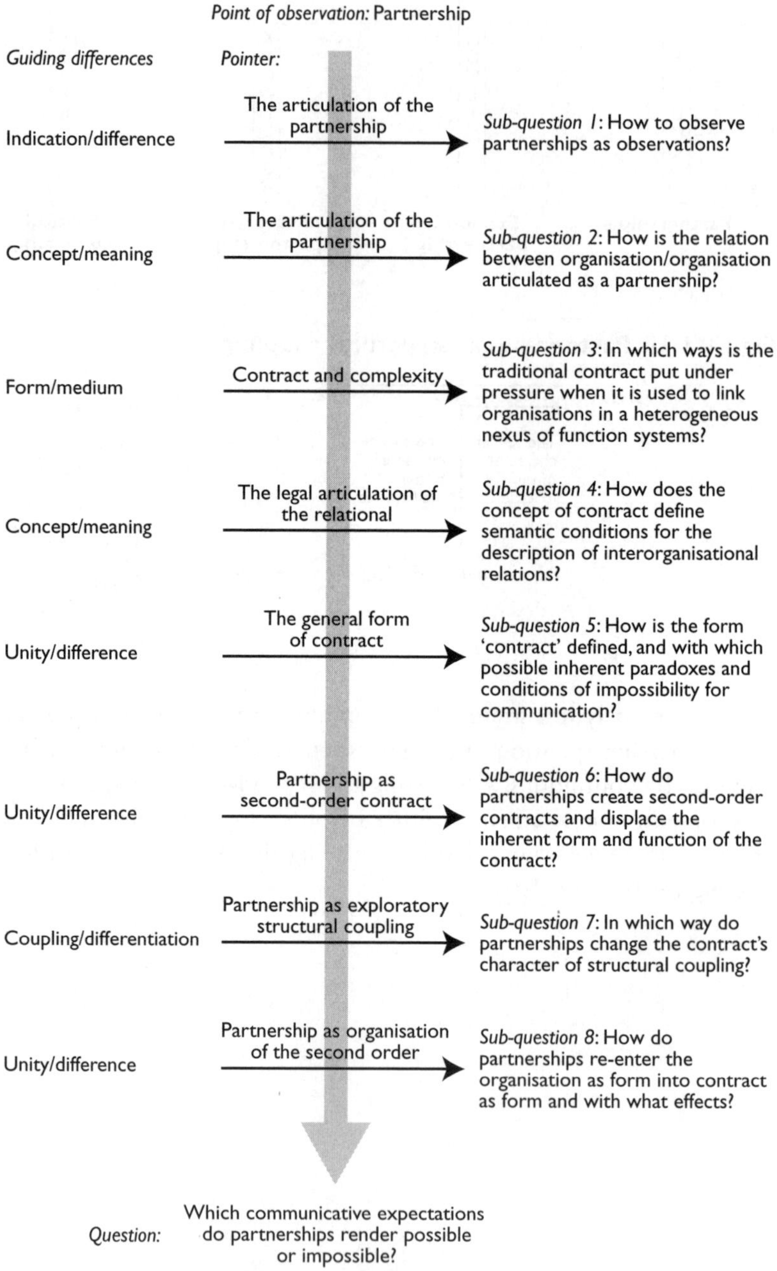

Point of observation: Partnership

Guiding differences	Pointer:	
Indication/difference	The articulation of the partnership →	*Sub-question 1*: How to observe partnerships as observations?
Concept/meaning	The articulation of the partnership →	*Sub-question 2*: How is the relation between organisation/organisation articulated as a partnership?
Form/medium	Contract and complexity →	*Sub-question 3*: In which ways is the traditional contract put under pressure when it is used to link organisations in a heterogeneous nexus of function systems?
Concept/meaning	The legal articulation of the relational →	*Sub-question 4*: How does the concept of contract define semantic conditions for the description of interorganisational relations?
Unity/difference	The general form of contract →	*Sub-question 5*: How is the form 'contract' defined, and with which possible inherent paradoxes and conditions of impossibility for communication?
Unity/difference	Partnership as second-order contract →	*Sub-question 6*: How do partnerships create second-order contracts and displace the inherent form and function of the contract?
Coupling/differentiation	Partnership as exploratory structural coupling →	*Sub-question 7*: In which way do partnerships change the contract's character of structural coupling?
Unity/difference	Partnership as organisation of the second order →	*Sub-question 8*: How do partnerships re-enter the organisation as form into contract as form and with what effects?

Question: Which communicative expectations do partnerships render possible or impossible?

TWO

Articulating partnerships

An initial path towards a diagnosis of the question of partnership was the *concept* of partnership as it is used by organisations. This chapter looks at the kind of communication that occurs around partnerships. How do partnerships become possible as the effect of particular semantic articulations of partnerships? Thus, we begin with a semantic analysis of partnerships.

In this chapter, therefore, partnership is observed as a particular semantics. Partnerships represent a semantics, that is, a reservoir of concepts that are currently available to an organisation for the description of and communication about interorganisational relations. An organisation observes itself, its environment and its relations to other systems in its environment through concepts, which in this way regulates what the organisation can and cannot see but also regulates the creation of expectations with respect to the organisation itself, its environment and to others.

What is interesting here is which observations and creations of expectations become possible through the concept of partnership? In which way do interorganisational relations become possible in the language of partnership? How do organisations come to observe each other when employing the conceptual reservoir that has formed around the concept of 'partnership'? What happens to the dimensions of time, fact and sociality in the language of partnership?

The analysis here focuses on how a partnership is formed as a concept, including the relation between concept and counterconcept. How and in which multiplicity is meaning condensed into the concept of partnership? What is established as concept and counterconcept respectively? Are there several terms for partnership where the concept remains the same? Are we able to observe different or possibly conflicting concepts of partnership in which the concept is the same but the counterconcept is different or in which concept/counterconcept are equivalents but where the meaning dimension is different? Or does the concept of partnership actually have the characteristics of an empty concept where there is an ongoing struggle about the ascription of meaning to it? Which rules of argumentation relate to the observation of the world through the concept of partnership? Generally, how is the formation of expectations organised in the partnership semantics?

A historical semantic analysis of the concept of partnership was intended; however, because the concept is being articulated within a large number of areas, it becomes an almost insurmountable task unless you choose to define one of the areas as exemplary of the history of the concept of partnership. This is often a good strategy and one previously chosen, for example, in a historical–semantic analysis of citizens' contracts where the author chose social policy as the point of observation (Andersen, 2003a). However, a central characteristic of the concept of partnership is precisely that it articulates relations across areas and sectors, which means that choosing a single sector as a point of observation would be highly inappropriate. Therefore, a different strategy has been chosen that transverses different fields. Five cases with different articulations of partnership have been selected, aiming for a level of heterogeneity with respect to who is articulating the partnership and with respect to the form of the partnerships. Thus, the analysis represents partnerships between public and private, between voluntary organisations and the public, as well as between different voluntary organisations across the boundary of industrialised nations/developing nations mediated by government development aid.

The five cases are all from Denmark but they are not specifically Danish; it is important to be aware of the relatively high flexibility and innovation capacity in the Danish welfare state. Maybe nothing begins in Denmark but international innovations are often very quickly identified and realised in internal innovation and development projects within the Danish welfare state. In this way Denmark often functions as a European test bed for social innovations and technologies (Campbell et al, 2006). So the five cases are not chosen to represent Denmark in particular but to represent different international articulations of partnership within one European nation state.

Social partnership: a community of strategic innovation

The first example is the report, *The social partnership*, published by the Danish consultancy unit Mandag Morgen Strategisk Forum in 1995 (Mandag Morgen Strategisk Forum, 1995). Mandag Morgen represents a rather special institution, particularly in the period from about 1987 until 1997. It is a weekly news publication and a consultancy as well as the organiser behind several cross-sectoral strategic think-tanks. During its strongest periods, Mandag Morgen succeeded in taking advantage of possibilities for synergy between its three functions for mobilising new political and economic agendas. With representatives from different groups the think-tanks produced strategic and visionary reports. The consultancy unit translated these visions into specific user-financed development projects, and the weekly news publication translated the visions and projects into news production that was often followed up by the national press (Kjær et al, 2001).

In this case, a similar scenario applies, that is, the report in question was part of a comprehensive campaign involving all three aspects of its work (Hardis, 2001). The Ministry of Social Affairs and the Ministry of Finance as well as a number of municipalities and counties drew up the report. This alone indicates that the report was an attempt to mobilise multiple players around a new wide-ranging project. The report was followed by several other reports, conferences, government initiatives and institutional developments. In Copenhagen in 1997 an international conference was held entitled 'New Partnerships for Social Cohesion – International Conference on the Social Commitment of Enterprises'. The conference led to the publication of a report with the same title, published by the Danish National Institute of Social Research and the Ministry of Social Affairs (Ministry of Social Affairs, 1997). In 2000 another report was published, entitled *It concerns us all: Status year 2000 for the campaign about corporate social responsibility* (Ministry of Social Affairs, 2000a). This described how the 1995 report from Mandag Morgen was in the process of being translated into specific initiatives and institutional development, including preparing municipalities to initiate close cooperation with companies. This pertains to the development, for example, of a concept about so-called open contracts between a municipality, local collective organisations and individual companies in which the company provides the municipality with job training and internships (Ministry of Social Affairs, 2000a, p 17). It also includes the effort to form national networks for business management, a national social index for the comparison of companies' social responsibility, social responsibility awards, and so on (Ministry of Social Affairs, 2000a, pp 28-9, 2000b, 2000c). And subsequently, many of these new ideas became incorporated in an agreement between state and local government, which appealed, moreover, to local government to employ so-called 'social clauses' in relation to outsourcing and the purchase of services. These imply that municipalities present service providers with specific social requirements. The appeal not only included private companies but also other organisations that the municipality supported financially, for example, sports organisations (National Association of Local Authorities in Denmark et al, 2000).

The social partnership pointed to a social challenge that cut across the difference between marketplace, civil society and state. The challenge was to not only create better conditions for the weakest in society but also to create the best possibilities for individual companies to develop. Thus, the report created a link between the fate of the weakest in society and the fate of private companies.

Companies were invited to rethink their strategies. The absence of social responsibility in companies resulted in an increasing number of legislative restrictions. Therefore, whether or not they wanted it, the working conditions of companies were linked to the wellbeing of the weakest in society. On the other hand, social involvement by the companies could increase both their productivity and competitiveness. Thus, a company acting in a socially responsible way was not defined in contrast to sound economic judgement. They are two sides of the same coin and it is from this perspective that the role of business in society has to be revised.

One of the many figures included in the report describes a social partnership as a place where market, state and civil society overlap, boundaries are crossed and intersections are established (see Figure 2.1).

Within these boundaries, a shared definition of social responsibility can take form in the cooperation between the involved parties pertaining, for example, to the upgrading of employee qualifications, improvement of working conditions or illness prevention (Mandag Morgen Strategisk Forum, 1995, p 66).

Figure 2.1: Partnership as an intersection

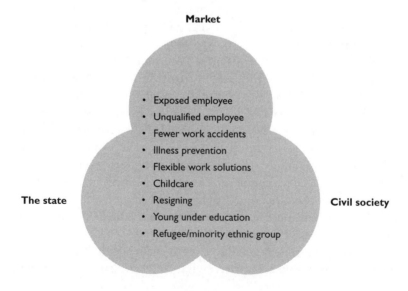

Market

The state

Civil society

- Exposed employee
- Unqualified employee
- Fewer work accidents
- Illness prevention
- Flexible work solutions
- Childcare
- Resigning
- Young under education
- Refugee/minority ethnic group

Partnership is defined as an alternative to sectoral break-ups. But it is also defined as an alternative to increasing government regulation and to the continued production and externalisation of social problems. Sectoral break-ups create a vicious cycle in which companies project social problems on to society, which increases government social spending and causes them to impose extensive welfare regulations. This puts further new burdens on companies in the form of taxes and increased regulations. The alternative that partnership provides consists of a shared space for strategic innovation within which the involved parties develop social involvement and act in a socially responsible way. Voluntary participation in partnerships makes it possible to collectively solve a number of problems and challenges and thus to avoid new government regulations and to break this vicious cycle (see Figure 2.2).

Figure 2.2: Mandag Morgen's partnership concept

Concept	Counterconcept
• Social partnership	• Sectoral break-up
• Collectivity	• Absence of social responsibility in companies
• Strategic innovation	
• Social involvement	• Increased regulation
• Collective social responsibility	• Increase of social problems

In this way, the concept of social partnership is defined positively as a collective space across the boundaries of societal sectors. The collective space represents a shared destiny because the alternative is much worse: collectivity means putting positive restraints on one another through shared goals for development. The absence of collectivity means putting negative restraints on one another in the form, for example, of increased government regulation of the private sector and more social responsibilities transferred from the private sector to the public sector and voluntary organisations.

Partnerships from the perspective of voluntary organisations

The next example addresses partnerships between voluntary organisations and public authorities from the perspective of voluntary organisations. It is a partnership description drawn up by the Centre for Voluntary Social Work (Center for frivilligt socialt arbejde). The

Centre refers to itself as a national centre working to support and promote voluntary work in Denmark: 'Our work is based on the ideal of a diverse and independent voluntary sector, contributing to the welfare society in cooperation with the public' (Center for frivilligt socialt arbejde, 2004, p 15).

The Centre for Voluntary Social Work seeks to provide voluntary organisations with a partnership concept and tools for their self-description in their partnership with public organisations in particular and also in part private companies. What follows is an analysis of the partnership semantics in the report *Partnerships between voluntary organisations and the public in the social field)* (Center for frivilligt socialt arbejde, 2003). The Centre for Voluntary Social Work repeatedly returns to this report in much of its work and so it represents a central point in their conceptual development in relation to partnerships.

The report formulated a dual problem of self-description. The Centre sought both to prescribe how an organisation could describe itself as voluntary and also to describe how a voluntary organisation could describe itself as in partnership with non-voluntary organisations without losing its voluntary character – how it was possible to work collectively with 'the other' without becoming like the other.

According to the Centre for Voluntary Social Work, therefore, you have to start by describing the distinctive features of the voluntary organisation. This description begins with a historical account of voluntary organisations in the modern welfare society.

The welfare state was initially established with an entirely coordinated and professional public system, which took 50 years. However, the notion of an all-encompassing public sector fell apart in the mid-1970s because of:

> dissatisfaction with common structures in the welfare state and their conventional solutions. The public system, which ensured an equal and uniform treatment of citizens from the south to the north, was seen as rigid, inflexible, and above all intrusive.[...] Citizens wanted more influence in relation to their lives and living conditions, which came to be reflected in the many alternative solutions that were developed, eg through the feminist and environmentalist movements. Similarly, many illness, handicap, and self-help organizations were founded in this period. (Center for frivilligt socialt arbejde, 2003, pp 1-2)

Thus, many voluntary organisations were created *spontaneously*; however, the real transformation did not begin until the 1980s, when the former

Minister of Social Affairs Ritt Bjerregaard confronted the public sector and appealed to grassroots organisations to take responsibility: 'By including other social-political actors to a much greater extent, the goal was to create a welfare society characterised by diversity and shared responsibility' (Center for frivilligt socialt arbejde, 2003, p 2).

Partnerships emerge here as the liberating force that could connect voluntary organisations with the public sector and transform the welfare state into a welfare society: 'In this context, partnerships between the public, private and voluntary sectors have been seen as a central tool, because partnerships produce new possibilities for development both in relation to the specific social service and in relation to the organisation surrounding it' (Center for frivilligt socialt arbejde, 2003, p 2).

This narrative is structured more or less like a classical fairy tale in Propp and Greimas' definition, in which the good old welfare society is disrupted by a poor economy and new expectations about individual control over people's lives. Voluntary organisations then appear as helpers, contributing to bringing the welfare state back home and on track. In the meantime, however, home has become a different and better place. It has been transformed from state into society (see Figure 2.3).

Figure 2.3: The fairy tale about welfare and voluntary organisations

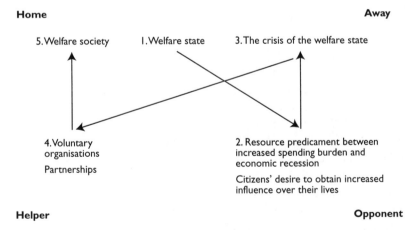

Home   **Away**

5. Welfare society   1. Welfare state   3. The crisis of the welfare state

4. Voluntary
organisations

Partnerships

2. Resource predicament between
increased spending burden and
economic recession

Citizens' desire to obtain increased
influence over their lives

Helper   **Opponent**

In the historical narrative, everything associated with the welfare society is defined as a positive future while everything associated with the welfare state is defined as a negative past.

Figure 2.4: From welfare state to welfare society

Future	Past
• *Welfare society*	• *Welfare state*
• Diversity	• The state as provider
• Collectivity	• Conventional solutions
• Partnership	• Equal and uniform service
• Equal cooperation across boundaries	• Rigid
• Influence over own life	• Inflexible
• Responsibility	• Intrusive
• Mutiple contributors to solution	• Distant
• Voluntary organisations as partners	• System
	• Sole provider of welfare services

Present
The moment of transformation

The present is the moment of transformation where the creation of partnerships can help us improve the future that has already been laid out for us in the form of the good welfare society with diversity, flexibility, collectivity, empowerment and inclusion.

Inherent in this narrative is another interesting narrative. It is not only the welfare state that is transformed into a welfare society; a transformation also takes place of the voluntary organisations themselves, a transformation that enables them to partake in the welfare society as an essential productive force. Before the quote above from the former Minister of Social Affairs with the magical words about the welfare society and collective responsibility, the text speaks about *grassroots* and *movements*. The text later refers, however, merely to voluntary *organisations*. It is a story of maturation, distinguishing between the spontaneously established grassroots movements of the 1970s, working independently in relation to the welfare state, and voluntary organisations as mature professional organisations, carrying a collective responsibility in the welfare society. Thus, voluntary organisations do not come into being unless their voluntary effort is, at the same time, tied to social responsibility. The text conceives of a form of symbiosis between the welfare society and voluntary organisations, a form of general contract by which voluntary organisations are only considered voluntary if they voluntarily tie and organise their voluntary efforts in relation to the responsibilities of the welfare society.

Consequently, partnership becomes a central concept. The concept of partnership indicates the possibility of the symbiosis. Thus, partnership does not simply represent a tool among numerous other tools. It specifically represents the mode of cooperation that is able to carry out the general welfare society contract. The reason that the partnership concept becomes so meaningful is that it promises to carry the notion of 'voluntary organisations in the welfare society': 'a partnership represents a mode of cooperation but contains many more elements of structure and responsibility than the simple fact that two organisations work together' (Center for frivilligt socialt arbejde, 2003, p 2).

Before giving a specific definition of the partnership concept, the report defines and outlines voluntary organisations. It does so by means of Figure 2.5, which it borrows from sociologist Lars Skov Henriksen (who in turn has borrowed it from Victor Pestorf).

Figure 2.5: Definition of voluntary organisations

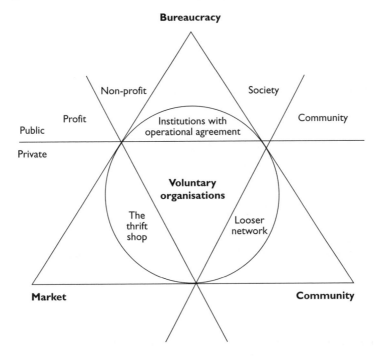

Voluntary organisations are not bureaucratic, not market-based, and not community-based. In other words, voluntary organisations are non-sector-specific. They are described as private and non-profit-oriented and characterised by goal rationality. Having said that, however, the description opens up since voluntary organisations can also cut across these boundaries and have marketisation, bureaucracy and community. A voluntary organisation may function more or less like a private company and still maintain its status and character as voluntary.

Following this typology of organisations, the report sought to typologise 'collaborations' according to the same model, so that 'collaborations' could be seen as bureaucratic (now referred to as hierarchical), market-based, or community-based (now referred to as network). And where are partnerships placed? Precisely in the space where voluntary organisations were before. Hence, voluntary organisations and partnerships are described as being 'made of the same stuff' (see Figure 2.6).

Figure 2.6: Definition of partnerships

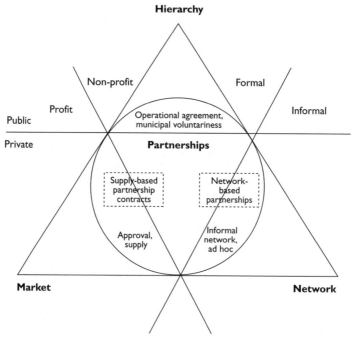

Partnerships are described as the ideal mode of collaboration characterised by equality, dialogue-based collectivity, trust and respect, and this ideal is maintained in a threefold negation of subordination, spontaneous collaboration and simple relations of purchase and sale. The concept/counterconcept structure of partnership is shown in Figure 2.7.

However, partnerships can be a result of a number of different sectoral logics, which leads to yet another distinction, one between demand-based and network-based partnerships. Both are described as possessing the general characteristics of partnership, but the ways in

Figure 2.7: The threefold negation of partnership

Concept	Counterconcept
• *Partnership*	• *Hierarchical collaborations*
• Collaboration characterised by equality, dialogue-based collectivity, trust and respect	• Hierarchical relationship
	• Assimilation of the partner
• Dialogue community	• *Market-based collaborations*
• Common development activities	• Purchase and sale relation
• Equal influence	• The aim is specific and well defined
• Structured and binding collaboration	• *Network-based collaborations*
	• Ad hoc
	• Spontaneous
	• Informal and low structured

Partnership concept

which they have been formed are different. They can either be based on spontaneous cooperaton or they can be based on demand. This means that voluntary organisations may under certain conditions also orient themselves towards public outsourcing to the extent that the contracts are given certain qualities. In this way, voluntary partnerships offer themselves up as medium for the political creation of welfare markets (see Højlund, 2004). Partnerships cannot, however, emerge from a hierarchical command. This means that cooperation between municipality-based voluntary organisations and the municipalities become excluded from obtaining the status of partnership. The distinctions are shown in Figure 2.8.

Figure 2.8: Supply-based and network-based partnership

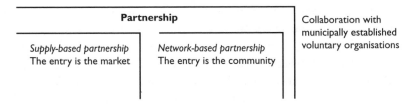

Partnership		Collaboration with municipally established voluntary organisations
Supply-based partnership The entry is the market	*Network-based partnership* The entry is the community	

As a whole, this creates a semantic in which voluntary organisations can describe themselves in relation to other organisational forms: they can describe the nature of their voluntary efforts, the nature of different modes of collaboration and the kind of collaboration that best matches the nature of voluntary organisations. Finally, this semantic enables the description of partnerships as the very medium that links together voluntary organisations and society in a realisation of the future welfare society.

Partnership 2000 and the strategy for civil society

The next example of the articulation of partnerships concerns partnerships between different voluntary organisations across the boundary of developing countries and industrialised nations, with financial support from the Danish state.

In 2000, the Danish Parliament adopted a new strategy for the use of development aid. The strategy was named Partnership 2000. Since then, the concept of partnership has been central to Danish policies concerning development aid, particularly partnerships between Danish non-governmental organisations (NGOs) and NGOs in developing countries. The focus on such partnerships is closely related to the desire to strengthen what Danida (Danish International Development Assistance) refers to as civil society in developing countries. In 2000, Danida published the *Strategy for Danish assistance to civil society in developing countries – Including collaboration with Danish NGOs. Analysis and strategy* (Danida, 2000a). It made a distinction between state, market and civil society and defined civil society as 'organisations through which citizens organise, which lie between the State and the individual family, and which is not part of the marketplace' (Danida, 2000a, p 8). Among these organisations, said Danida, are also informal self-help groups, traditional organisations and local women's groups. Danida believed it could find among the civil society organisations 'an organised expression of the interest of poor population groups, and organisations which work to maintain a democratic development and which are capable of partaking as a continual contribution to and challenge of the State with respect to the development or further development of a democratic government. These are the forces on civil society which Denmark wishes to support and strengthen' (Danida, 2000a, p 12). Danida summarised their interest in civil society organisations as follows: 'Therefore, it is through the collaboration with groups in civil society that we can create popular participation in the development process and that poor and marginalised men and women can be heard' (Danida, 2000a, p 12).

Partnerships between what is referred to as 'western NGOs and their sister organisations in developing countries' are emphasised as a central way to strengthen the above-mentioned civil society organisations. With respect to partnerships, Danida says: 'The background for Partnership 2000 [...] is that it is possible and imperative to establish realistic partnerships on the basis of a recognition and shared understanding of inequalities and different backgrounds on the one hand, and an agreement about shared goals and visions and the formulation of mutual responsibilities on the other. Thus, the partnership concept represents a goal and a vision for how the collaboration should develop while also recognising and respecting the differences' (Danida, 2000a, p 33).

Danida was aware that the conditions for dialogue between Danish NGOs and their sister organisations in developing countries were impeded by an asymmetry whereby Danish NGOs were seen as better resourced and government funded (Danida, 2000a, p 25). Therefore, they encouraged both parties to present objectives and value bases to each other and to engage in a dialogue about them. This made backgrounds and expectations visible and able to be discussed for the future partner. Moreover, Danida put great emphasis on the so-called 'capacity development' of the partners in the developing countries. They wrote: 'The responsibility of the Danish NGOs should be to support capacity development of their partners in the developing countries with a view to enabling them to represent the interests of their members and to assume the role of advocate and take on relevant development activities' (Danida, 2000a, p 50). The report goes on: 'It is important that support for capacity development is based on the partner's own visions and established objectives. Capacity includes in particular the ability to carry out lobbying and advocacy activities so that the partner can articulate and promote their own needs and interests' (Danida, 2000a, p 50).

It is an interesting partnership concept that is outlined here. Emphasis is placed on the dialogical qualities of the partnership and on the immediate equality inherent in the reference to partnerships between Danish NGOs and sister organisations in developing countries. Subsequently, however, the report recognises the asymmetry between the partners and assigns to the Danish NGOs the role of transforming their sister partner into an equal partner. Thus, the report assumes that the asymmetry will be levelled out by defining the already stronger partner as the one who is to *create* the other weaker partner as a stronger partner. In this way, the Danish NGO is assumed to be working on both sides of the partnership. The report states: 'An ideal partnership is not established from one day to the next. It requires time, patience, and a shared vision to strengthen the inadequately resourced partner' (Danida, 2000b, p 15).

This role as capacity builder is emphasised by Danida when they write that partnership projects intended to provide services such as farming consultancy should fundamentally be about capacity development:

'Ultimately, these projects should always be carried out in relation to capacity development and advocacy activities so that the target group – impoverished men and women – obtains increased political capacity and ability to influence the structural reasons for poverty, marginalisation, and the lack of equality between the sexes' (Danida, 2000a, p 53). Or as Danida wrote in a subsequent report: 'A project providing access to services for poor populations can strengthen the credibility and local framework of the local NGO, hence creating a strong basis for advocacy activities' (Danida, 2004a, p 3).

Throughout this capacity development strategy, Danida considers it a central effort to select and form NGOs in developing countries since there is no guarantee as to the popularity of the sister organisation and they may not represent the poor in an appropriate way. The central principles of Danish development aid are equality, environment, democracy and human rights (Danida, 2000a, p 50). NGOs in developing countries also need to be created as partners, in Danida's view: 'Denmark will seek to support groups, which work, through formal and informal channels, to achieve a democratic process of change that benefits the poor' (Danida, 2000b, p 14).

This creates an interesting new partnership dilemma – Danish NGOs should meet the same requirements as NGOs in developing countries. If Danish NGOs are to help create NGOs that actually represent the poor in the developing countries, they ought to be popular. This question is discussed in a report from Danida in 2004 entitled *The popular anchorage of Danish NGOs* (2004b). The report encouraged Danida to follow the development and popular nature of Danish NGOs and to form contracts with the individual NGO that include objectives for people- and community-based anchorage. The report says: 'Most [NGO] organisations consider themselves "popular" to varying degrees defined on the basis of their self-perception and constituted through the particular origin, history, objective, focus, and member base of the individual organisation. Few organizations have worked strategically and systematically with "popular anchorage" but most consider popular appeal a constituting characteristic feature' (Danida, 20004b, part 2, p 23). A central concept becomes 'the operationalisation of popular appeal', comprising both the profiling and contractualisation of popular appeal.

The report included a comprehensive analysis of the popular anchorage of a number of Danish NGOs. These include DanChurchAid, Ibis, MS Danish Association and Save the Children Denmark. The analysis presented diagrams, curves and graphs covering individual organisations' popular profile, voluntary work, involvement of volunteers, membership development, and so on. Its aim was to encourage increased dialogue with the NGOs about popular anchorage and Danida saw it as its role to formulate specific demands on individual NGOs (Danida, 2004b, part 1, p 15). For example, in relation to MS Danish Association, Danida concluded:

> Continued growth in individual membership will be given special consideration in the evaluation of the popular anchorage of MS Danish Association and will work as an important parameter in assessing Danida's support for the activities of MS Danish Association over the coming years. At the beginning of 2005 – once the total membership numbers have been calculated at the end of 2004 – Danida will discuss separately with MS Danish Association the organisation's efforts and results in this area and possible implications for the level of funding. (Danida, 2004b, part 1, p 18)

Altogether, this creates a partnership concept in which the state, according to Danida, observes partnerships between Danish NGOs and NGOs in developing countries as a medium for the creation of civil society in developing countries: partnerships, that is, which are primarily around building partners. The responsibility of Danish NGOs in establishing partnerships is to contribute to the capacity development of NGOs in developing countries into relevant and strong partners. Employing a combination of dialogue and economic incentives, Danida's role is to ensure that Danish NGOs are able to appear as partners of popular anchorage for the sister organisations in developing countries. Partnerships create partners, we might say.

ISS Denmark and Hørsholm Hospital: a public–private partnership

The next case involves ISS Denmark and Hørsholm Hospital. ISS is a multinational facility service group operating in 47 countries. It has more than 350,000 employees and was founded in 1901 in Denmark.

The partnership description of ISS Denmark and Hørsholm Hospital represents an entirely different point of observation. Their partnership is a so-called public–private partnership (PPP). This section looks at the way in which the takeover by ISS Denmark in 2002 of all non-clinical service functions at Hørsholm Hospital was described as a partnership with the hospital. Hørsholm Hospital described the partnership as different from outsourcing – outsourcing was seen as establishing a conflict of interest between customer and supplier whereas a partnership 'creates a clear focus on the shared responsibility of Hørsholm Hospital and ISS Denmark to create patient satisfaction' (Hørsholm Hospital, 2002). It is a question of assuming what is referred to as a shared responsibility, which is able to meet 'our vision to be a hospital for the patients' (Hørsholm Hospital, 2002). Hørsholm Hospital outlines the partnership as shown in Figure 2.9.

Figure 2.9 is composed of three circles. At the centre are responsibilities such as cleaning and patient food. The next circle is described in terms of the quality of service as flexibility, dialogue based and behaviour. The outer circle is the partnership, forming the context for how to understand and carry out services and responsibilities. The partnership is described in terms such as shared responsibility, shared projects, shared organisational culture, shared values, mutual acceptance, loyalty, and so

Figure 2.9: Hørsholm Hospital as depicted by the hospital as partnership

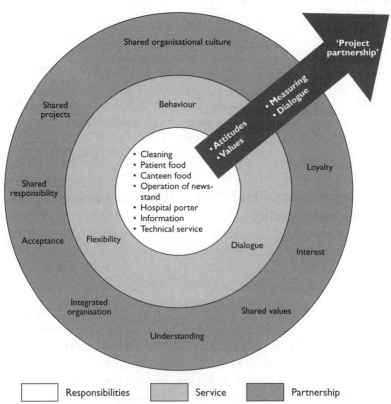

on. In the direction from the centre pointing outward is an arrow with the heading 'project partnership', with the sub-headings 'attitudes', 'values', 'measuring' and 'dialogue'. The arrow stresses the fact that the partnership is perceived dynamically as something that is continually evolving. The content of the partnership can develop over time.

Partnership is defined in contrast to a contract. It is not, it is said, so much a legal construction as an attitude towards the collaboration of assuming shared responsibility for the overall development of the hospital. The partnership is indicated as a second-order promise: it is a promise about how the involved parties are going to respond to the promises about responsibilities and services.

Towards the end of the partnership description, there is another reference to outsourcing as different from partnership:

> Often a picture is worth a thousand words, and even though the comparison only goes so far, the difference between outsourcing and partnership is comparable to the difference between paying for sex on the one hand, and love on the other. Paying for sex is a "commodity" where the interest of the buyer and the supplier are entirely different and where one supplier can be exchanged with another without difficulty. Love on the other hand refers to a relationship in which two people enrich each other in shared development. And as in love, a partnership requires openness and trust in order to succeed. (Hørsholm Hospital, 2002).

Elsewhere, ISS Denmark writes about its partnerships with hospitals:

> Partnerships are based on mutual trust and shared responsibility rather than contract and control as in traditional outsourcing. In the partnership model, the tender documents can be limited to a single binder because the specific collaboration and service agreement is not developed until the partners have 'chosen' each other and have sat down together around the table. Another central aspect of the partnership idea is that the parties assume shared responsibility. Neither customer nor supplier is able to disclaim responsibility. (Søndergård, 2003, p 407)

This concept of partnership is summarised in Figure 2.10.

Contract and outsourcing are defined in clear opposition to partnership. Partnership establishes ties that indicate something greater, deeper and more long term than a contract. At the same time, however, it seems apparent that partnerships are also formed with a

Figure 2.10: Hørsholm Hospital's concept of partnership

Concept	Counterconcept
• Partnership	• Pure outsourcing
• Love	• Paying for sex
• Established relationship	• Exchangeable partners
• Complete confidentiality	• Entirely different interests in the transaction
• 'Chosen each other'	• Strict customer–supplier relationship
• Shared value base	
• 'Almost no boundaries'	
• Shared responsibility	• Contract
• Shared projects	• Control
• Shared company culture	• Limited responsibility
• Mutual acceptance	• Exchange value
• Mutual respect	• Egotism
• Loyalty	• Closedness
• Openness	• Mistrust
• Trust	

view to establishing contracts about specific services. These are called agreements. This creates a peculiar constellation because contracts are perceived as something that gets in the way of contracts. We need a partnership in order to have contracts. First, we choose each other and commit to a collective space, then we form agreements within that space in which we act as people whose interests in the agreement and transaction are different but still within a shared space (see Figure 2.11).

Figure 2.11: The social order in the partnership concept for Hørsholm Hospital

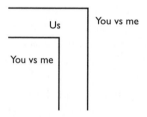

The partnership is defined as an 'us' and not as a 'you vs me'; an 'us' that is also seen as the precondition for 'us', that is, 'you and I', to appear as 'you vs me' and consequently to enter into specific negotiations and agreements with each other without ending up in mistrust, trench warfare and conflict.

There is also a particular form in relation to the temporal dimension. The distinction between partnership and contract represents a distinction between two forms of temporality. A contract represents a short-term form that is abandoned once the contract no longer meets the interests and objectives of the individual parties. Partnerships are not short term, however, but they also cannot be called long term. Hørsholm Hospital presents the partnership as almost eternal. Once established, it has always existed and will always exist. What is bounded in time is the collective value about a good hospital. Such values do not suddenly cease to exist. It is clearly an expectational structure that does not anticipate a divorce in the process of developing the partnership. But in the eternal relationship, contracts may function as brief relationships that the parties repeatedly leave behind. In the eternal relationship, agreements can be made to leave each other.

In this concept of temporality, the temporal dimension becomes repeated in communication. Making an agreement in the future means to describe what the parties are to deliver in the future. Forming a partnership as described above, on the other hand, means to describe in the present a shared future which might hold many presents that describe singular future exchanges in reference to the shared future. Or, more specifically, on the temporal dimension, partnerships are about presentiation of future presentation of the future.

The consultancy AS/3's partnership model for the labour market

The last example is the description by the consultancy AS/3 of its vision for itself in a partnership with the National Labor Market Authority and the public employment exchange in a municipality. They, too, define outsourcing in opposition to contracts. Outsourcing is seen as transitory contract periods characterised by stop–go relations. It entails great risk of conflict, sub-optimal quality and discontinued collaboration. The consultancy formulates it like this: 'Conflict may arise because the task is complex. We are dealing with highly dynamic material in a fluctuant world. One can be certain, therefore, that some things will change once the work begins' (AS/3, 2003a, p 3). Partnership is considered a positive alternative: 'If on the other hand one chooses the partnership model, the situation is different from the beginning. Partnerships typically imply a more long-term contract period. The relation between public and other providers is based on mutual trust and continual dialogue. And a management team representing the involved parties are in charge of the project' (AS/3, 2003a, p 3). As in the last example, AS/3 favours circle figures (see Figure 2.12).

Figure 2.12: AS/3's partnership figure

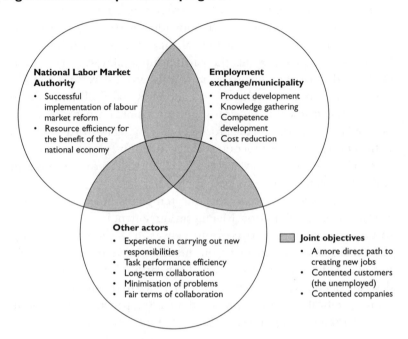

The figure shows three intersecting circles. Each circle indicates an interested party with its own interests, objectives and perspective. The focus of the National Labor Market Authority is successful implementation of labour market reforms and resource efficiency. The focus of the employment exchange is competence development and cost reduction. The focus of the provider companies (for example, AS/3) is task performance efficiency and long-term collaboration. The intersection is defined as shared interests and objectives, for example, satisfied customers and companies. Thus, a partnership is characterised by intersecting interests derived from intersecting shared objectives, which means that the joint project can be developed under changeable conditions based on mutual trust and continual dialogue.

Again we see a figure that contrasts partnership and outsourcing (see Figure 2.13).

However, there is also another figure that is about complexity and time. Partnerships claim to be about relations so complex that they cannot be handled through outsourcing. It is this complexity that increases the above-mentioned risks. According to AS/3, this complexity functions on two dimensions: on the factual dimension where the task is more complex than what can be described in the contract, and in particular on the temporal dimension with reference

Figure 2.13: AS/3's concept of partnership

Concept	Counterconcept
• Partnership	• Outsourcing
• Long-term contract periods	• Stop-go relations
• Mutual trust	• Risk of conflict
• Continual dialogue	• Risk of sub-optimal quality
• Joint management group	• Risk of discontinued collaboration

to a fluctuating world in which the premises for collaboration are constantly changing.

Conclusion

As we can see, the partnership concept is expected to comprise quite a few elements. These examples of how to give meaning to the concept of partnership indicate that there are a great number of expectations linked to partnerships and that many different types of organisations are associated with partnerships. It seems that there is a multiplicity of meaning condensed into the concept that creates an expectational horizon of dimensions. Partnerships are expected to represent an alternative to outsourcing, an alternative to sectoral break-ups, an alternative to state, market and civil society as well as a way to bridge these, the answer to topical problems in the welfare state and its transformation into welfare society, an adequate way to establish commitment in a complex and changeable society, a way to open up public markets, and a way to engage in developmental politics in the developing world which empowers local NGOs to be able to develop on their own (see Figure 2.14 overleaf).

The concept of partnership brings a great number of issues into play at once. It articulates the self-relation of the organisations, relations between organisations, the relation between organisation and society, the relation between decision and time, the relation between individual and collectivity, the relation between different sectors in society such as state and market and, finally, the relation between contract and commitment. At the same time, partnership is defined as the horizon for the development of the welfare society. Partnership is in itself something good. And at the same time it is a tool for development in developing countries, a synergy between public and private and for the opening up of public markets.

Figure 2.14: Partnership as the condensation of a multiplicity of meaning

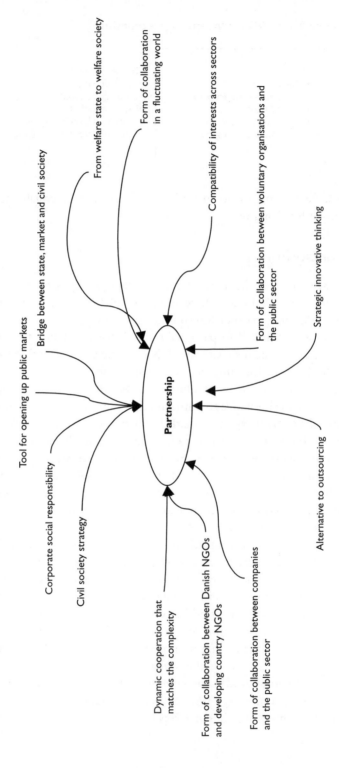

All in all this constitutes an impressive chain of equivalence, which seeks to equate a large number of semantic elements with each other. Such a chain can only be held together if the many different elements are similar in their difference from something else, that is, if one counterconcept is able to organise the common negations of the conceptual equivalents. This counterconcept appears to be outsourcing and contracts.

The concept of partnership seems to provide a semantic for organisations' description of their interorganisational relations. The examples of articulations of partnerships share ideas of:

- cross–sectoral work
- collectivity
- dialogue
- agreement under evolving circumstances
- project orientation
- a focus on future and visions.

These ideas are all defined in opposition to the more short-term contractual relation. Partnerships seem to be precisely what a contractual relationship is not: not short term, not characterised by narrow self-interest, not mistrust, and so on.

However, there are also significant differences in the articulation of partnerships as a solution:

- *Time:* in the case of AS/3, the temporal dimension has highest priority in the articulation of partnerships as a solution. The main problem is defined as having to collaborate under constantly changing conditions. Here, contracts become problematic because they are unable to handle temporal complexity. Contracts are incompatible with constant change and development, which is why partnerships are seen as a solution.
- *Case:* in the case of Hørsholm Hospital, on the other hand, the factual dimension has highest priority. Here, the main problem is described as the factual complexity of the collaboration. The contract is unable to reflect the complexity of the services, which is why they have chosen partnerships, something that indicates the values behind the services.
- *Social:* finally, in the case of Danida (as well as the case about voluntary organisations and that of Mandag Morgen) the social dimension has highest priority. Here, the main issue is described as the social asymmetry of the collaboration. Contracts require mutual partners of equal standing, which is not the case, and hence partnerships

become the way in which one party assumes responsibility for the construction of the other as an equal partner.

The way that contracts move along their own limits is the subject of the next chapter.

THREE

Outsourcing limits

Having observed the way in which the partnership concept is made available to organisations' internal communications about their interorganisational relations, the way that different systems of communication collide in the development of outsourcing and contracts across the public and private sector will now be discussed.

The starting point is a distinction between organisational systems and function systems.

Organisations are defined as social systems that communicate through decisions. They are in a certain sense decision-making machines that create themselves through decisions and consist therefore of nothing but decisions and decision premises. Organisational systems are fundamentally exclusive; you are excluded from the organisation unless the organisation decides to include you through the assignment of membership.

Function systems are defined as social systems that are based in society and are functionally closed around themselves through the use of specific media. Function systems are systems such as, for example, the political system, the legal system, the economic system, the religious system, the arts system and the mass media system. These are all characterised by communicating in each of their symbolically generalised media; the economic system of communication forms money as a medium, the political system forms media as a medium and the mass media system forms information as a medium.

The communication media are referred to as symbolic because they are concentrated around a few clear symbols. In the economic system of communication, the medium is money and the symbols coins and notes.

Furthermore, symbolically generated media are *general* in the sense that the medium can be employed to communicate about anything. It is not tied to specific situations. For example, anything that can be symbolised through money can be communicated about economically.

Finally, all symbolically generalised media establish *binary codes* for communication. Binary codes divide all communication into plus and minus values. The positive values define a fundamental striving or motive in the communication, although they do not specify the motive. The negative value in the code serves as a calibration value.

If the communication employs a binary code, it can be seen by the fact that the communication is only able to be continued with either plus or minus.

Moreover, the fact that the code is binary means that it divides the world into two. The entire world can be perceived from the perspective of the code. The medium of money, for example, implies the code to have/not to have by which it is naturally better to have than not to have. The entire world can be summed up in this code. Thus, if communication links up with a symbolically generalised medium, it is only able to link up with either the plus or minus side. There is no third value. This also means that two media cannot be communicated at once. If you link up through the economic code, everything is perceived economically. If you link up though the legal code, everything is perceived legally. The codes represent perspectives, so to speak, which exclude each other (Luhmann, 1992b). Each of the codes represents a total logic, and changing the code transforms the communication's entire content and possibilities for continuation.

Function systems are societal systems, which, unlike organisational systems, are not closed around membership. In principle, everyone is able to partake in the communication of a function system. Partaking in the economy does not require a particular status. One person's money is as good as another's. But economic communication causes the world to appear in a specific way.

Society can be seen, therefore, as differentiated into a large number of function systems, each with their symbolically generalised medium and binary codes or logics, which preclude communication between function systems. Figure 3.1 illustrates this; it does not, however, comprise all existing function systems. In Figure 3.1 function systems are placed next to each other to emphasise the fact that there is no ranking order and also no centre that can represent society as a whole.

Figure 3.1: Function systems and their media and codes

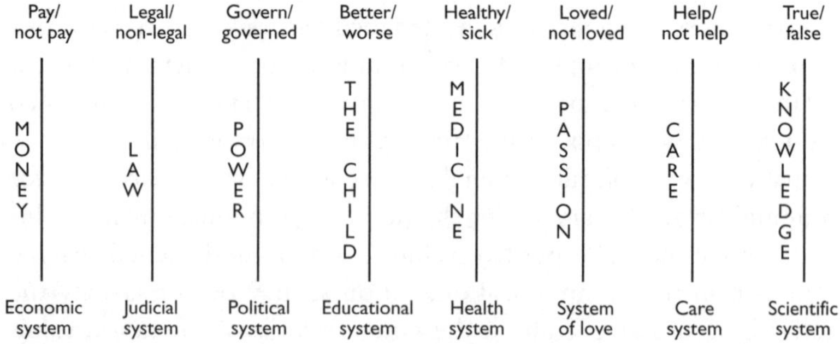

Pay/ not pay	Legal/ non-legal	Govern/ governed	Better/ worse	Healthy/ sick	Loved/ not loved	Help/ not help	True/ false
MONEY	LAW	POWER	THE CHILD	MEDICINE	PASSION	CARE	KNOWLEDGE
Economic system	Judicial system	Political system	Educational system	Health system	System of love	Care system	Scientific system

There exists no super-code that may unite the many codes into one perspective.

Unlike the function systems, organisational systems do not have their own symbolically generalised media in the same way that they do not have their own binary codes. Rather, organisational systems operate with a horizon of decision premises, which precisely opens up for the diversity of the encodings. Moreover, decisions cannot even be communicated in organisations without forming the media of the function systems. This does not turn the function system into a sub-system of the organisational system, but it establishes a structural coupling between function system and organisational system within the organisational system. Thus, organisations and function systems constitute each other's environment, but organisational systems are always linked to at least one function system by reaping the benefits of its symbolically generalised medium (see Figure 3.2).

Figure 3.2: The relation between function system and organisation

Traditionally, even though an organisation always employs several different codes, they have a primary codification. In parallel to the differentiation of the function systems, organisational forms have evolved, adapted to the individual function system with structures that provide for the codification of that specific function system. Thus, we normally identify the different function systems by means of organisational representations rather than by means of their media and codes. We identify the healthcare system as the field of hospitals, clinics, private practices, and so on, the economic system through organisations such as companies, banks and stock exchanges, the political system through political parties and parliaments, and so on.

Homophonous organisations will be discussed in this context. A *homophonous organisation* is defined as an organisation that is primarily linked to one function system and has, therefore, a primary codification that regulates when other codifications may be relevant. This means that the code that the organisation chooses to form when describing and programming itself remains stable. The time of initiation of a given code in a homophonous organisation is structurally fixed. The organisation is internally differentiated in a way so that sub-systems may be differently encoded without this resulting in the clash of codes. Notions of distinct professions with independent decision competency may be part of such a structure (Andersen, 2003b; Andersen and Born, 2003).

One example could be a traditional party political organisation. Such organisations primarily form the medium of power and are coded, therefore, in govern/governed and government/opposition. Self-programming takes place in the form of political programmes. They regulate their membership limit politically, and so on. But the organisational communication also forms other media. The party forms the medium of money to the extent that there is an existing economy and therefore also decisions about economic prioritisations. However, in the homophonous party, the discussion of programme never develops into economic communication whereas the opposite is possible, that is, for economic priorities to become politicised. The party also forms the medium of law to the extent that it operates under specific legislation, for example, with respect to eligibility, financial contributions, presentation of accounts, and so on. Another example could be a private company that has a primary economic codification but that also forms the legal code, for example, in its work with contracts.

The homophonous organisation is illustrated in Figure 3.3 opposite. The function systems are differentiated side by side and without ranking order each with their function, medium and code. The organisational systems emerge in their coupling with the function systems so that particular organisational forms relate to the different function systems that are designed to form their particular medium. Thus, homophonous organisations have a primary functional coupling.

As we will see later, outsourcing drives private companies and public providers in the direction of what is referred to here as *heterophony* or *polyphony*. The development of organisations from homophony to heterophony means that a growing number of organisations no longer hold a primary coupling to a single function system. There is no longer one predominant relation between organisational type and function system, or in terms of organisational theory. There are no longer unambiguous expectations regulating the selection of premises in the decisions. A growing number of organisations form codes

Figure 3.3: Function-specific homophonous organisational forms

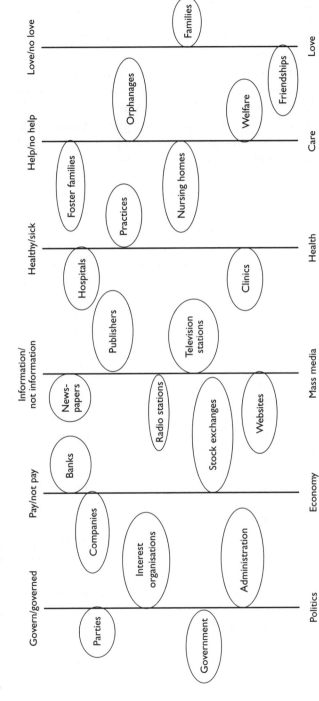

without a hierarchical relationship among them. The relation between an organisational system and function system is one of contingency, and what is 'new' is that it is perceived as such in the organisation. An organisation is defined as heterophonic when it is linked up with several function systems where there is not one function system that can be predefined as primary. Therefore, there is always a plurality of codes available and no horizon of premises to regulate the choice of coupling (Andersen, 2003b, 2004a; Andersen and Born, 2003).

From the point of observation of the organisation, heterophony means that an increasing number of media are available to an increasing number of organisations. Not only are the media available to communication about specific functionally delimited themes but also to the organisation's overall self-description. The heterophonic organisation cannot choose to departmentalise their coupling to a number of function systems to concern only organisational sub-systems. Therefore, another distinctive feature of the heterophonic organisation is that it continually seeks to establish a primary codification. In other words, it has to constantly make decisions with respect to the choice of medium of communication and the medium through which communication is to continue is never predefined. These choices are crucial since the symbolically generalised media have binary codes that initiate both their motivational and reflectional values. Whenever the code changes, it also changes the perspective on the decision, on the organisation and on the world outside. Thus, the heterophonic organisation is one in which incomparable values clash and in which no value is able to capture and represent the totality of the others. Any attempt to install such a super-value will always merely increase the polyphonic complexity. The super-value is bound to fall into place alongside the other values and thereby simply add yet another coupling to a new function system with a new medium and a new code. Creating and recreating its horizon of premises constitutes the basic strategic challenge of the heterophonic organisation.

This chapter goes on to illustrate the way in which communications clash when organisations with couplings to a variety of different function systems have to collaborate. It concerns complexity management in contractual relations across different systems of communication and the way in which the traditional contract is put under pressure when employed to connect organisations with very different function system attachments.

We start with a case concerning the outsourcing to ISS Catering of the provision of meals for older people in the municipality of Lyngby-Taarbæk (the case is described in depth in Andersen, 1996, 2000).

The case begins in 1990 when ISS Denmark offered a free analysis of the provision of meals for older people in Lyngby-Taarbæk. The analysis concluded that outsourcing the kitchens operation would mean great possibilities for rationalisation and public cost reductions. In 1992 the municipality decided to go ahead with the outsourcing and hired a consultancy to advise them about the call for tenders. The winner of the contract was ISS Catering, and the company took over the municipality's kitchens at the beginning of 1994. However, it was not a smooth takeover. As soon as the staff changed into ISS uniforms and ISS cars replaced the municipality's cars, complaints started to be filed by older people and relatives about the food and food delivery. In the months to come, the complaints kept pouring in and political conflicts started to form.

Until 1990, the municipality's social committee had never discussed the provision of meals for older people. In 1995, the committee held 12 meetings, which all featured the provision of meals for older people on the agenda. Until 1992, the committee on older people and people with disabilities had never discussed the provision of meals for older people. In 1995, the committee held 10 meetings where the provision of meals was part of the agenda. Until 1992, the local press had never written anything about the provision of meals for older people; in 1995, there were 16 articles.

We see the emergence of a peculiar field (see Figure 3.4). The field consists of the municipality with its hierarchy and functional divisions, ISS with its hierarchy, IMM as the consultancy hired by the municipality to file a monthly report concerning ISS's compliance with the contract, local and national media, and so on. Communication appears to be moving in all directions between the organisations in the field. The

Figure 3.4: The policy field (in the case of meals for older people)

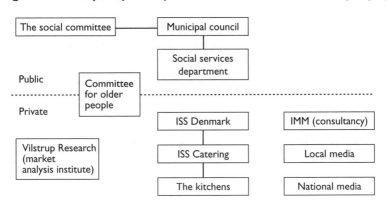

reports from IMM about contract compliance resulted in meetings of the social committee, which led to meetings of the committee for older people demanding that action be taken by the social services department that then instructed ISS Denmark to act in particular ways. ISS Denmark, IMM and the social services department exchanged letters full of sharp reciprocal accusations. The opposition asked the mayor for numerous reports about the case. The municipal council put the operations of ISS Denmark on their agenda and the media reported from the meetings. Vilstrup Research was hired to work out an objective analysis of the satisfaction among older people with the food. The report was perceived by the media as adding to the conflict, as an indication of lack of control in the municipal council and as an input to improving the performance of ISS Denmark. Subsequently, the municipal council set up a committee of prominent members to test the food, including the social services director. The committee ate at different nursing homes every week and reported back to the social committee, which subsequently placed ISS Denmark on all its agendas and demanded even more regulation. The story keeps evolving.

For example, IMM, who were hired by the municipality to monitor the contract, wrote a status note about the collaboration with ISS Catering A/S: 'We are clearly of the opinion that ISS Denmark expresses the right attitudes in writing and orally, however, when these ideas have to be put into practice in day-to-day activities, the agreements appear to be "empty rhetoric" – without actual content' (quoted in Andersen, 1996, p 105). ISS Denmark provided a very different interpretation of the events, here in an internal letter from the managing director of ISS Catering to the group managing director of ISS Denmark:

> It has become apparent that there continue to be vast differences between entering into a business agreement with a politically controlled unit and a private organisation. The political form of governance does not allow for that which the politicians express a desire to achieve, that is, flexibility, possibilities of placing the users [older people] at the centre, etc. Instead, this form of governance is focused on political control which cannot be converted into flexible and dynamic business agreements. (quoted in Andersen, 1996, p 112)

ISS Denmark watched the case of ISS Catering in Lyngby-Taarbæk and its potentially damaging effect on the image of the entire group through, for example, television reports. On that basis, ISS Denmark chose to back out of the deal.

In their notice of termination ISS Denmark wrote:'1. *The managerial authority* has not as determined in the contract been with ISS Catering. 2. *The involvement of a consultancy* has not been conducive to the collaboration. 3. *The conditions for payment for additional services* have not been observed' (quoted in Andersen, 1996, p 112). ISS Denmark also submitted its notice of termination to the local media, which gave rise to a fallout about the course of events. Kaj Aage Ørnskov, then mayor of Lyngby-Taarbæk municipality, made the following comment on ISS Denmark's contract termination:'ISS has found it difficult to cope with the harsh criticism, also in the media. This is of course damaging to a company. On the other hand, the fact that the political debate in a municipality takes place in public and on premises different than when two companies do business with each other should not come as a surprise to a private company' (quoted in Andersen, 1996, p 113). IMM consultancy also felt called on to comment on ISS's termination of the contract:'The role of IMM has been clear from the beginning – also to ISS Catering – that is, as "watchdog" concerning compliance with the contract agreement [...] ISS Catering has not demonstrated the ability or willingness to enter into actual dialogue and cooperation about the actual problems with IMM or the employees of the municipality' (quoted in Andersen, 1996, p 114).

We might ask: how did it happen that a well-planned outsourcing project, involving an experienced and professional catering company and a well-organised municipality supported by a consultancy with special competencies in contract formulation and administration, ended up in such uncontrollable conflicts?

Much research from Britain based on experiences with the outsourcing of public services indicates that this is not a unique case. Neu speaks of the irony of contractualisation, which refers to the fact that effective outsourcing of responsibilities in the form of contracts requires an environment of trust. However, the mere introduction of contracts tends to undermine such trust (Neu, 1991). Seal and Vincent-Jones are not quite as unambiguous, but they still provide documentation for the fact that short-term contracts tend to undermine relations of trust. Outsourcing can, in particular, create a climate of mistrust, particularly in combination with a Taylorian regulatory spirit (Seal and Vincent-Jones, 1997). However, the theoretical discussion seems to be characterised by the conception that long-term relations are sustained by trust and that trust is essentially entirely different from a contract. This creates a strange figure in which a formally established partnership is imagined to be held together precisely by that which evades the contract. You can enter into formal partnerships, but maintain at the same time that what makes partnerships unique is the fact that they are not contractual collaborations (see, for example, Vincent-Jones and Harries, 1995). This seems an insufficient theory and an indication of fundamental flaws in the theory about what constitutes a contract.

The diagnosis of the problem is that cross-sectoral collaboration entails couplings between systems of communication that are essentially unable to communicate with each other, and that this enhances the potential for and risk of conflicts.

The case of ISS Denmark in Lyngby–Taarbæk municipality involved at least three functional systems of communication in addition to the many organisational systems. First of all, there was the political system. This is a system of communication that communicates through power and forms two related codes: govern/governed and government/opposition (the latter code reflects the fact that democratic forms of governance divide the governing position into two). Lyngby–Taarbæk's outsourcing of responsibilities to ISS reflects a governance decision and subsequently ISS is observed by the municipal administration in the same way as any other performing unit, that is, as governed; the municipality governs, ISS is governed. The political system of communication entails a continual struggle to occupy the governing position and this struggle divides the world into government and opposition where all communication supports the effort to gain power (somewhat simplified, on a municipal level this means winning the mayoralty and majority). An often quite effective strategy is for the opposition to show how the current governing majority does not have a firm grip on things. This is also the strategy employed by the minority in Lyngby–Taarbæk municipality, which is further supported by the fact that the municipality received a monthly report from the consultancy IMM about ISS's various neglects in relation to the contractual agreement. Naturally, any dereliction of duty is seen by the opposition as the mayor's inability to govern. Subsequently, the mayor was forced to take decisive action and to show his willingness to govern by publicly reprimanding ISS as if the company were a subordinate and disobedient administrative organ.

In addition to the political system of communication, the case also involved an economic system of communication. This communicates through money, thereby forming the code to have/not to have (or, in a more active form, to pay/not to pay). In economic communication, the entire world is divided into what someone has and what someone else does not have, where it is obviously seen as better to have than not to have. When you have something, you implicitly have it at your disposal. Whereas governance is the fundamental motivating value in political communication, having represents the fundamental motivating value in economic communication. ISS primarily link up with the economic code. To them, the decision to take over the municipal kitchens was not a governance decision but first and foremost an economic decision indicating that it made good business sense both to ISS and the municipality for ISS to run the kitchens. Within this logic, outsourcing implies that ISS subsequently have the kitchens at their disposal. They hold the managerial authority. Thus, when the mayor and the municipal administration reprimanded ISS as if they were governed, it simply does not make sense to ISS. The company does not see itself as part of the municipal hierarchy but as an independent organisation, which happens to now also include some municipal kitchens. To ISS, the inquiry only makes sense as a disagreement about payment, not as a reprimand to a subordinate. Thus, it is clear to both municipality and company that a disagreement exists; however, the conception of the type of disagreement was not and could not be the same.

Finally, there was the mass media system. Mass media communicate through the medium of information and divide the entire world into information and non-information. In this way, mass media communication is like a large editorial machine, constantly sorting and construing information, which is then passed on. The story contains all that a journalistic heart can desire in terms of conflict material. And since the local events could be related to and made symptomatic of national controversies about outsourcing, the future of the welfare state, and the greed of large companies, local news was quickly transformed into national news.

At the same time, there was little if any reflection of the fact that the case involved many codes for communication. The communication was characterised by a mono-contextual conception of the world just as it appeared. There was no conception of other observers with other perspectives to whom the world might look different. The municipality, the political parties, the consultancy and ISS all believed they saw the world the way it really was. They each had their own perspectives. And the same was true for the contract – the contract was what it was and there was one and only one correct interpretation of it.

The result is that contradictions were transformed into a self-contained conflict system independent of the conflict parties. It led to the establishment of a conflict system based on the logic 'whatever harms the others benefits me'. The conflict became self-contained so that the conflict itself recruited new themes for new conflicts. Failure to deliver biscuits on Sunday, leaking packaging at Ms Jones's, too much pepper in the gravy, staff cuts outside the agreement. Nothing was too small or too big for yet another meeting in the municipal council. None of the involved parties had any control over the conflict and no one could stop it or give it direction. Instead, the conflict consumed more and more attention from all parties.

The partnership in Lyngby-Taarbæk failed, but many of today's outsourcing projects and partnerships entail even greater internal complexity. The partnership between Hørsholm Hospital and ISS Denmark puts at least six systems of communication into play, each of them seeking to communicate about the events in their own code: the political system, the economic system, the healthcare system, the care system, the mass media system and the legal system. They each seek to adopt their individual perspective on the events in and around the hospital, perspectives that can under no circumstances be summed up in totality. AS/3's partnerships comprise the political systems (which in this case even becomes differentiated into state and municipality, both of which seek to contend for the top position), the economic system, the educational system, the care system, the mass media system and the legal system.

The point is that public outsourcing produces a multitude of value clashes across the board of different function systems. At the same time, the very form of outsourcing provides no framework within which the conflicts can play themselves out. And it is this complexity that so-called cross-sectoral partnerships have to match.

FOUR

Contracts and relationality

This chapter provides a shift in analytical perspective as well as point of observation. Having carried out a semantic analysis of the partnership concept and of the way in which it both opens and closes in a particular way the possibility for organisations to communicate about mutual relations, and having provided a case analysis of communication clashes across function systems in a public outsourcing project, this chapter now provides a semantic analysis of contract semantics in legal theory. Preliminary analysis indicates that the traditional contract is being put under pressure in cross-sectoral collaborations. Legal contract theory is included in this book because the legal system has most consistently nurtured the concept of contract and has developed a language for and around it.

A discussion of whether and how legal contract theory forms concepts that can be said to be equivalent to the partnership concept and to collaborations involving many function systems follows. In other words, from the perspective of contract theory, does the traditional concept of contract seem to be put under pressure? In which ways has the discussion of contract law sought to solve the complexity questions? In which ways has the discussion of contract law formulated questions about trans-boundary contracts, communication and complexity? We will observe the way that the legal contract-theoretical language allows for the description of interorganisational relations as well as interfunctioning of systemic relations.

This chapter does not provide a review of every discussion in this field, but simply highlights three 'clusters' of theory. The first is Ian R. Macneil's theory about *relational contracts*. Macneil clearly opens up for question the impact that communication has on contract formation. He also formulates a question about complexity management in contracts. His goal is to bring society into contract development itself as an extra-contractual element. The second is Stewart Macaulay who, in addition to having an eye for the question of communication, opens up a kind of perspectivism in the understanding of the *specific life and interpretation of contracts*. The third is the discussion of *reflexive elements in contracts*. This discussion finds inspiration in the writings of both Macneil and Macaulay, but also has references to a more normative discussion of welfare law and to Gunther Teubner's systems theory about reflexive law. This cluster is highly heterogeneous and includes people like Hugh Collins, Peter Vincent-Jones and Peter Campbell. Its concern is to find new answers to contemporary contractual problems but it is reluctant to endorse a more fundamental change in the understanding of contracts. Thus, three openings are maintained for communication, perspectivism and reflexivity respectively. However, it is also argued that the discussion of contract law continues to refrain from viewing contracts as one form of communication among a great number of other systems of communication, and this significantly hampers its capacity for understanding the problems illustrated by means of the ISS case mentioned in Chapter Three.

Ian R. Macneil: the concept of the relational contract

Ian R. Macneil's two most significant works were the article 'The many futures of contracts' (1974) and the book *The new social contract* (1980) (see also Macneil, 1985, 1987, 1988, 2003). What impels Macneil to formulate a new contract theory is his observation of the fact that the conditions for contractual relations have been fundamentally changed due to growing societal complexity. Modern contracts are seen as:

> intimately interconnected with a larger society of great complexity, involving extremely complex specializations of labor and product, and always subject to constant change.[...] Modern contractual relations too tend to involve large numbers of people, often huge numbers of people.[...] The modern contractual relation too tends toward long life. Many, especially large groupings, have beginnings shrouded in the past.[...] Many such relations also take on and shuck off new members, some for all their working life, while the relations themselves continue. Finally, all of these modern relations, large and small, demand future cooperation not only in performing what is planned but in future planning. (Macneil, 1980, pp 20-1)

Macneil's focal point seems to be a distinction between contract and society, and the answer to the described complexity challenge to include society in the contract. However, it requires a great number of theoretical displacements in order to comprehensively argue this point. It requires, for example, for society to *always already* be *in* the contract, albeit to different degrees, and it requires a communications-theoretical conception of contract as text in context. This alone becomes rather complex, but we restrict ourselves here to a relatively simple analysis of his figure of argumentation.

Overall, Macneil perceives the relationship between contract and society as follows:

> Contract without the common needs and tastes created only by society is inconceivable. Contract between totally isolated, utility-maximizing individuals is not a contract, but war: contract without language is impossible; and contract without social structure and stability is quite literally rationally unthinkable, just as man outside society is rationally unthinkable. The fundamental root, the base, of contract is society. Never has contract occurred without society; never will it occur without society; and never can its functioning be understood isolated from its *particular* society. (Macneil, 1980, pp 1-2)

Therefore, contract is always in society. It is defined as a legally sanctioned promise, and a promise is fundamentally seen as a particular form of communication: 'Present communication of a commitment to future engagement in a specific reciprocal measured exchange' (Macneil, 1974, p 715). Contracts, Macneil argues, represent a 'projection of exchange into the future' (Macneil, 1974, pp 712-13). Thus, promises become a question of a presentiation of the future. This is what all promise communication is about: for the communication parties to install the future in the present as the premise of acting in the present. This, however, is a difficult operation because it means to speak about and specify what does not yet exist. Macneil argues that whereas the present can be specified and communicated, this does not apply to the future towards which a promise is directed. A promise, therefore, becomes a strange thing: 'Promise in transactions is simply specified communication of what for us goes without saying' (Macneil, 1974, p 719).

A promise, writes Macneil, 'is an affirmation of the power of the human will to affect the future. It affirms that an individual can affect the future now' (Macneil, 1980, pp 6-7). It is precisely this temporal function of the contract that becomes constitutive of the social character of the promise. A promise both binds and individualises freedom. It individualises it by installing the participants of the promise communication as individuals with freedom of action for binding their freedom. It binds by reducing the individuals' future dispositions:

Thus, the first two elements of promise in its contractual
context are the will of two or more individuals with beliefs
in the power of one to affect the future – subject to the
linkage of the social matrix essential to exchange. A third
element of promise is the doing of something now to limit
the choices otherwise available to the promisor in the future.
This is part of the notion of commitment encompassed in
the Restatement definition. For example, a person entering
an agreement to sell a house no longer may choose to sell it
elsewhere without suffering the consequences of breaching
his promise. These may be as intangible as a loss of reputation
or as concrete as a judgment awarding damages. (Macneil,
1980, pp 6-7)

Promises, however, represent incomplete communication: certain limits
apply to the presentation of the future as the premise for individual
present and future action. First of all, promises are condemned to being
fragmentary: '*Promises are inherently fragmentary.* [...] *Thus, promises can
never encompass more than a fragment of the total situation*' (Macneil, 1980,
p 8; emphasis added). It is about the fact that attention is always limited
– you are unable to focus on everything. This also applies to promises
that consequently become fragmentary.

Second, sent communication is not the same as received
communication: 'a promise made and a promise heard are two different
things', writes Macneil (1974, p 728). Thus he adopts a first-order
cybernetic perspective on contract. He implies that communication
consists of A coding and sending a message, which B receives and
decodes and that coding and decoding do not necessarily coincide. In
fact he points out that they can never coincide, which has dramatic
implications for the possibility of promise. He formulates it like this:
'Every promise is always two promises, the sender's and the receiver's'
(Macneil, 1980, p 9). This means giving up the unity of the promise:
'When differences between saying and hearing occur, [...] there is no
way in which the future of the promise can be viewed as identical in
all respects to the present world of reality because in present there are
two promises, declarer's and hearer's, and with them *two* contradictory
futures, and both cannot be brought into a single present as present'
(Macneil, 1974, pp 728-9).

The problem is how promises become possible when they seem
impossible. Macneil's answer falls in two parts. The first is that promise-
based exchange presupposes non-promise-based exchange. The order of
promise is defined as dependent on an order, which is not constituted
by promise. Macneil tells us that there are a number of alternatives

to the promise as exchange projector such as tradition, status, habits and hierarchical commandoes. Then he adds that these alternative exchange projectors often exist side by side with promises (Macneil, 1980, pp 6-8). And finally he argues, 'promises have always been accompanied by burdens of impurities of incompleteness of content, and communication, objectivity, implication, custom, usage, and above all, "ongoingness" and its accompanying clouds of imprecision and future uncertainty' (Macneil, 1974, p 731). He adds: 'Promise, even at its transactional narrowest, always is shadowed by non-promissory accompaniments' (Macneil, 1974, p 731). This adds up to a peculiar figure that makes the possibility of promise dependent on non-promises: 'Once promises are viewed as less than absolute, other exchange-projectors inevitably must come into play' (Macneil, 1980, p 9). This is summarised in Figure 4.1.

Figure 4.1: Macneil's relationship between promise and exchange

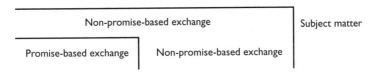

Figure 4.1 illustrates Macneil's attempt to solve a paradox about the impossibility of promise by folding it into yet another paradox in which the distinction between promise and non-promise is placed in a context of non-promise. Having established this figure of argumentation, the distinction between promise-based and non-promise-based exchange is replaced by a distinction between discrete contracts and relational contracts. Discrete contracts are defined as a transactional relation that is impersonal and without duration. Discrete contracts represent pure promises, pure transactions characterised by the fact that, apart from the exchange, no relations exist between the parties. Hence they are also called transactional contracts (Macneil, 1974, pp 721-6). Relational contracts, on the other hand, are defined as personal and permanent (Macneil, 1974, p 721). They establish relational relations that comprise whole persons, deep communication and non-economic personal fulfilment (Macneil, 1974, p 723).

This makes it possible to construct a continuum of contracts with the transactional and relational respectively as the two outer poles. Contracts can be more or less relational and transactional, more or less personal, more or less deep.

However, with reference to the above-mentioned quote about contracts always being in society, Macneil argues that even the most discrete contracts have to be relational. His assertion is that any contract, however discrete, involves relations and hence has to be relational (Macneil, 1980, p 10). This is due to the fact that society is fundamentally viewed as relationally constituted. This gives us another paradoxical basic figure (see Figure 4.2).

Figure 4.2: The re-entry of relationality into itself

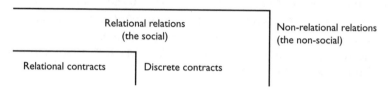

Discrete contracts are not relational relations that occur in the relational. Society is fundamentally relationally constituted and discrete transactional contracts are not. Thus, discrete contracts come to represent a form of occurrence of the non-social in the social on the terms of the social.

All these conceptual twists serve a purpose, that is, to provide an answer to the prefatory problems with respect to contracts under conditions of high societal complexity: 'But what has that to do with modern contracts? This query brings us to the concluding part of the chapter in which we shall focus on modern contractual relations' (Macneil, 1980, p 22). The point is simply that transactional contracts presuppose simple, stable and calculable surroundings. The complexity of new technology alone dissolves this presupposition and requires relational contractual elements (Macneil, 1980, pp 22-4). The greater the complexity the greater the support for the relationality of non-relational contracts: deep communication, whole persons, non-economic motivation and personal relations provide the answer to differentiation and complexity. And where do we recognise this figure from in practice? In the topical partnership rhetoric where the dividing effect of traditional contracts is to be moderated and suspended by mutual proclamations of collectivity, values and 'matrimonial love'.

Stewart Macaulay: the perspective-dependence of contract

Like Macneil, Stewart Macaulay takes a communications–theoretical approach to contract law, but he adds a form of perspectivism that expands the question of the possibility of fixing the promise.

We begin, however, by presenting the communications approach in its closest proximity to that of Macneil. In his article, 'The real and the paper deal: empirical pictures of relationships, complexity and the urge for transparent simple rules' (2003), Macaulay looks at contracts from a communications perspective. It is, however, a very different communications perspective from Macneil's. To Macaulay it is not simply a question of sending and receiving a message about a promise. Rather, it is a question of the contract as some kind of nexus between a flow of communication participants:

> Those who negotiate the deal often are not the people who draft the written document recording it. Still others must perform the contract. This opens the possibility that, for example, a firm's lawyers may have different assumptions and expectations than its purchasing agents, sales people and engineers. Strategy may be involved too. If I want a clause that says if event X takes place, then consequence Y will follow, you may demand something in exchange that I do not want to give you. When I anticipate this, it may be better to avoid raising the issue in negotiations and hope that the matter can be resolved if event X ever takes place.[...] In short, there are many reasons why the paper deal will fail to capture the real deal. As a matter of fact, there is a 'text between the lines'. (Macaulay, 2003, pp 54–5)

What Macaulay means by 'real deal' is: 'both those actual expectations that exist in and out of a written contract and the generalised expectation that a trading partner will behave reasonably in solving problems as they arise' (Macaulay, 2003, p 54, note 6). What Macaulay opens his study of contract law up towards is the discussion of formation of expectations in contract communication, both in the development of the contract as well as in the contract's many communicative afterlives. This has consequences for the understanding of contracts:

> Contracts are always more than the contract document. We have long known the many reasons for this: words do not have a fixed meaning that every speaker of the language will

translate the same way. We create the meaning of written language by bringing to the words some measure of context, background assumptions, our experiences, and, too often, our bias, ignorance and stupidities.[…] Also, it is very hard to bring the future to the present and provide that X will happen if event Y takes place. Our ability to predict the future is limited, and even careful business people often leave gaps in written contracts. The world changes and surprises us: Wars break out in places where we do not expect them; or our contract may have dealt with a war but left open what happens when the direct effect of a major terrorist attack makes performance much more costly; OPEC drives up energy costs unexpectedly; new technologies, often involving computers, change things so than an older contract no longer makes sense. Even when we can foresee that it is possible that something might happen, there are limits on the time that we can or should spend on trying to provide for all contingencies in our contracts. (Macaulay, 2003, pp 53-5)

Unlike Macneil, Macaulay is highly aware of the fact that contract communication is not simply communication between different individuals with different intents. It is also communication between different perspectives of the world, represented in Macaulay by professions. Macaulay is very aware of the internal differentiation of companies in particular functions with appertaining professions. This interest and focus date back to the early 1960s. As early as 1963, Macaulay illustrated in a number of interviews that different people thought about very different things when referring to a contract. He also implied that people's thoughts were tied to their different roles in the company: salespeople, financial workers, purchasing agents and lawyers (Macaulay, 1963a, pp 13-40). Business people prefer to believe someone's word even when a transaction involves serious risks. Lawyers in turn often speak with regret about this attitude. Macaulay refers to a quote from an interview with a lawyer: 'Often businessmen do not feel that they have "a contract" – rather they have an order. They speak about "canceling the order" rather than about "breaching our contract"' (Macaulay, 1963b, p 61). He also quotes a businessman: 'You can settle any dispute if you keep the lawyers and accountants out of it. They do not understand the give-and-take needed in business' (Macaulay, 1963b, p 61). Macaulay concludes that detailed contract planning and legal sanctions played a crucial role in some exchanges. However, in many business exchanges these only played a minor role: 'To understand the function of contract, the whole system of conducting exchanges must be explored fully' (Macaulay, 1963b, p 67).

In the 1980s, Macaulay expanded on his analysis. He showed, for example, how written contracts in companies were given very different weight. Business people and sales personnel preferred a word for a word. They 'are more concerned with emphasizing contract compliance than with planning what happens if problems arise such as unforeseen expenses or non-delivery, in the same way that they also do not ensure that their contracts are legally binding' (Macaulay, 1963b, p 60; 1987, p 91). Lawyers, attorneys and budget managers were more focused on the writing of contracts, budget managers because the contract was seen as a management tool in relation to the various processes in a large organisation.

Macaulay pointed out that contracts were not an integrating factor – contracts were unable to join together the different professional perspectives because it would require a collective discussion of the contractual norms that would increase the risk of conflict even before negotiations really began (Macaulay, 1987, p 99; 2004, p 792). Instead, business people took part in an economic community in which it was assumed that relinquishments tended to be returned in the form of advantages. The economic community consisted of social relations across formal channels and entailed ample opportunity for sanctions. It was a social network that functioned as a system of communication. People told on each other and that created sanctions in the form of threats to someone's reputation (Macaulay, 1985, p 468).

In recent years, Macaulay has again expanded the frame of observation for contracts. A contract is not only translated differently by internally differentiated professions in contracting organisations; a contract's translation, assessment and sanctioning also depend on the social field to which the contracting organisations belong. Macneil's relational relations are now seen as being able to achieve independent status as a field, creating its own rules and binding obligations that are often more effective and stronger than national legislation. Macaulay speaks of 'private government' and argues that public authorities do not provide much regulation. Legally, it might be necessary to maintain a distinction between public and private, but in the real world this distinction does not exist (Macaulay, 1986, p 445). There is a need for a 'private regulatory perspective' that does not overestimate the distinction between public and private. Macaulay argues that the social fields become self-regulating private systems of regulation (Macaulay, 1991).

All in all, Macaulay has contributed immensely to contract theory with important empirical research about how contract development and employment actually take place, empirical research that does not only include purely legal processes in relation to contracts but also the many different professions that have to relate to contracts and exchanges in companies. In relation to Macneil, communication is no longer seen simply as something that takes place between isolated individuals. The background and particularly the professional roles of communication participants are viewed as an important aspect of the contract communication. Differences in the conception of contracts are no longer simply individually based but tied to different functions in the company, although it is also obvious that the functions and professions that Macaulay pays attention to are concerned with either economy or law exclusively. In relation to Macneil, Macaulay's empirical curiosity and realism means that even though he borrows many concepts from Macneil, including the distinction between transactional and relational contracts, they are not given the same normative weight. Macaulay's empirical interest and his general theoretical openness leads him in the direction of a great number of issues, but these are never given solid theoretical form. This applies to his observations of the fact that business people, lawyers and budget people view contracts differently. He never inquires into what constitutes the business person's view of contracts. What, for example, does the business person represent in Macaulay's decision to quote him? A random person doing business, a function, profession, a system, a notion? This remains very unclear, which is why his ideas never amount to an actual theory. Similarly with private government, he opens up to a very important question and provides empirical examples but never develops an actual theory about private regulation.

Hugh Collins, Peter Vincent-Jones and David Campbell: the concept of reflexivity

Over the past decade, we have seen the emergence of a discussion of welfare law that builds on the ideas of Macneil and Macaulay, often with a normative view to incorporate the insight produced by Macneil and Macaulay into contract development and contract law. One of the key concepts seems to be reflexivity. Hugh Collins, Peter Vincent-Jones and David Campbell have been the most prominent voices in this discussion. The chief work in this discussion is probably Hugh Collins' book from 1999 with the provocative title, *Regulating contracts*, provocative because it signals an abolishment of the distinction between public law and contract law. Another very important book is Peter Vincent-Jones's *The new public contracting* from 2006.

On the outskirts of this discussion of contract law and its reflexive elements we find Gunther Teubner. We return to a discussion of his work later, but in this context it seems relevant to mention Teubner as a systems theorist who for the past 30 years has studied the development of law, including contract law. He is the originator of the concept of reflexive law, and this concept plays an ambivalent role in the works of Hugh Collins, Peter Vincent-Jones and David Campbell. These writers are undoubtedly all inspired by Teubner's works; however, none of them subscribes to his communicative systems theory. We might say that they find inspiration in Teubner's models for solutions whereas they more or less radically oppose his problem formulation and methodology. It could be described as a Macneilian reading of Teubner. Teubner's theoretical works are seen as overly complex and theoretically excessive (Campbell, 2000a, 2000b).

This is a rather comprehensive and multi-faceted discussion. However, the central problem seems to be how to incorporate justice into contract law, including ensuring that contracts reflect more than the mere interest of the contractual parties (Collins, 1993). Campbell formulates it like this: 'What is needed to develop, at the heart of the law of contract, is a social self-consciousness of the necessary conditions of contractual justice' (2000a, p 490).

Collins defines the question in the following way: 'The general view seems to be that the law of contract does not embody as one of its aims the achievement of a particular pattern of distributive justice. […] The legal test for the formation of a binding contract merely establishes fair procedures by which individuals may reach their agreements; they do not ensure that the outcomes of the bargains conform to some fair distributive pattern of wealth in society. The law of contract purports to rest upon a platform of neutrality with respect to distributive outcome' (Collins, 1992, p 49). He seeks to find out why this is and whether it is really true that the involvement of the welfare state in fair reallocation does not influence contract law. He asks how it is possible to regulate the market without considering whether the welfare is distributed fairly or unfairly (Collins, 1992, p 51). Collins suggests a new concept for the description of pure procedures and argues that these should always meet three basic requirements: (1) they have to satisfy the participants as rational maximators; (2) they have to most effectively protect against the distortion of the negotiation outcome; and (3) they must be procedures that have been selected under the condition of fair opportunities (Collins, 1992, p 55).

In his book *Regulating contract*, Collins even suggests that both contract law and individual contracts should contain reflexive mechanisms. Private law ought to reinvent itself to make itself sensitive to many systems (Collins, 1999, pp 65-9; Campbell, 2000a, p 496).

Willie Seal and Peter Vincent-Jones also argue that outsourcing and public–private collaborations may benefit from incorporating reflexive elements into their contracts. Seal even refers to 'reflexive contracting' and public–private partnerships (PPPs) as couplings of closed systems (2000, p 15). Vincent-Jones speaks about the enormous expenses associated with the lack of reflexive mechanisms in contractual relations across the public–private boundary (1998, pp 371, 374; Seal, 1996). Vincent-Jones and Harries write that contracts can emphasise constructive collaboration (1996, p 191). In a subsequent article Vincent-Jones argues that regulatory regimes can be assessed in relation to measures of reflexivity and responsivity. An ideal for the reflexive regulation of the responsibility of public authorities for ordering and purchasing on the quasi-market has to include: (1) democratic and open development of regulations through negotiation with involved parties; (2) a cooperating non-hostile relationship between regulator and regulated party; (3) a high level of regulatory flexibility for the regulated party; (4) operational efficiency; and (5) result efficiency (Vincent-Jones, 1999, p 314). Responsivity might be achieved to the extent that different interests meet in the contractualisation process. A contract can be viewed as a mechanism linking ordering agent, executing agent and consumer in a way that leads to more or less responsive regulation of quasi-markets. It is easier for responsive regulation to be achieved when the regulatory regimes are themselves reflexive (Vincent-Jones, 1999, pp 310, 322, 2000, pp 317-51).

Vincent-Jones's latest book tries to make a full diagnosis of the contractualisation of the public sector, including PPPs, contracting out, internal contracting and contracts between government administrations and individual citizens. In his attempt to cover all the ongoing forms of contractualisation he goes beyond a purely legal point of view, studying contractual obligations that might be both legal and extra-legal. He makes two important sets of distinctions. He first distinguishes between the empirically observable behaviour of contracting, the rhetorical use of contract in political discourse and the recourse to contract terminology in our attempts to understand social relations (Vincent-Jones, 2006, p 10). This distinction is later substituted with a distinction between administrative contracts, economic contracts and social contracts. Administrative contracts are contractual arrangements intended to increase the transparency and effectiveness of governance in the public sector. They rely on values such as political accountability, good governance, separation of powers and the exercise of discretion. Economic contracts are contractual arrangements directed at improving public services through competition in a variety of hybrid forms beyond simple market or bureaucratic organisations such as PPPs. Economic contracts rely on values like distributive justice, public interest and efficiency. Social contracts are contractual arrangements in the regulation of relationships between individual citizens and the state authority and rely on values like justice, efficiency, protection of public interest, individual responsibility and rehabilitation (Vincent-Jones, 2006, pp 21-9). The distinction between these three forms of contracts is intended to indicate social functions and policy purposes rather than legal qualities (Vincent-Jones, 2006, p 21). So he is very aware of the extra-legal qualities of new forms of public contracting. Although he remains within the purview of legal description, in dealing with all these emerging forms of contractualisation he also expands the concept of responsiveness along a number of dimensions: (1) regulator sensitivity; (2) collaborative regulation; (3) restorative justice; (4) organisational learning; (5) institutional adaptation; (6) consumer and citizen needs; and (7) public accountability. These seven dimensions express a heterogeneous empirical–inductive analytical typology rather than a theoretical and systematic one (Vincent-Jones, 2006, pp 87-115). And again he insists on the extra-legal qualities:

> Responsiveness [...] cannot be reduced to law or regulation. Responsiveness is ultimately a product of specific governance arrangements.[...] Responsive or reflexive law may help secure the preconditions and determine the parameters of the operation of responsive governance. Responsive governance is founded at least to some degree on responsive law. However, responsive governance is dependent on organizational, economic, administrative and political arrangements that have their own existence and influence outside the ambit of law and legal norms. (Vincent-Jones, 2006, p 102)

Conclusion

As we have discussed, since the 1960s there has been a discussion of the relation between contract and society and contract and complexity management. The discussion has gradually opened itself up to questions that have not traditionally been included in contract law. The first such opening is to see communication as an aspect of contract formation. Macneil perceives this as all contract formation involving a problem with respect to successful communication of promises between contractual parties. This problem can never be entirely overcome because each of the communication parties has their own personal context for understanding. However, the problem can be lessened through relational relations between communication parties, relations that define shared norms and a mutually dialogical attitude.

The second opening consists of a form of perspectivism, primarily maintained by Macaulay. This perspectivism is constituted by observations of the fact that the appropriateness of the contract is fundamentally perceived differently from different positions in the company. However, it is a rather weak perspectivism. Macaulay sees that contracts are viewed differently from different perspectives but he does not see what determines these perspectives. He merely indicates these in statements such as 'the sales person believes', 'the lawyer on the other hand finds', and so on.

The third opening consists of bringing reflexive elements into contracts and in making contract law reflexive of non-legal considerations. This is a recognition of the necessity of incorporating Macaulay's perspectivism into the concept of contract itself. However, the discussion about reflection remains rather abstract and tends in many instances to become a community orientation along the same lines as Macneil. Reflexive mechanisms are defined as procedural participant involvement based on the notion of legal support of dialogue between interested parties. The concept of reflection remains an empty category without unequivocal content. There are frequent acknowledgements of different systems of communication but ultimately these become reduced to players in the capacity of 'bonus pater familias'. Despite the recognition of many systems, the contract is still consistently seen as precisely legal. At the same time, non-legal systems are merely indicated as non-legal. Their individual logics are never described and are not included in the discussion. The existence and importance of non-legal and non-economic systems are recognised as such but remain an indefinite mass of incomprehensible communication. The discussion acknowledges the existence of a great number of systems but fails to indicate them by employing the concept of procedure to disregard their specific characteristics.

It is as if Macneil cannot bear the cynicism of his own analysis of the impossibility of promise and has to therefore install hope. The result is a peculiar mix of communications-theoretical realism and communitarian collectivity romanticism.

On the whole, we see a number of openings into contract theory; however, these openings are neither radical nor do they have enough consequences to offer up a new theory, a new programme for observation, that matches the complexity surrounding partnerships. Thus, these openings often result in naïve oppositions of contract as the discreet relation whose possibilities under complex conditions have to be established through non-contractual collectively based partnerships. Non-agreements are to hold together agreements.

We are left with at least three problems:

- *An internal contract problem:* legal contract theory observes an increasing gap between the preconditions of the formal contract and conditions pertaining to contract formations in society.
- *An internal theoretical problem:* three approaches are employed in order to overcome the gap between the preconditions of the formal contract and the conditions of society: relationing, perspectivism and proceduralisation. However, the development of contract theory is impeded by the fact that it takes place within the distinction between action and language. From Macneil via Macaulay to Collins, there is an inherent presupposition that action is different from language. Entering a contract agreement is an action. Reading a contract is linguistic. These two entities are separated so that contract formation itself is neither seen as language nor communication.
- *An external contract problem:* moreover, the discussion persistently takes place within the distinction between law and everything else on the basis of the premise that there is in principle something outside the law. Nevertheless, the law continues to function as the neutral ground within which the discussions take place. And that basically means that the complexity of society is only represented in legal terms. There is no possibility for transcending the systems and developing an eye for the way the law is closed around itself. The law becomes naturalised as the ultimate place 'from which'. This also manifests itself in the discussion's implicit perception of the contractual parties. There is always the presupposition of some subjects outside the contract with the status of bonus pater familias that means that even the subject positions become naturalised in relation to contracts.

We might be able to find the solution to these three problems in Niklas Luhmann's systems theory, who defines communication as the fundamental event of the social. This will be pursued in the following chapters.

FIVE

Contracts as communication

The discursive openings from Macneil, Macaulay and Collins should be seen as fundamental rather than as a supplement to a dilapidated legal theory. First of all, contracts should be seen as a particular form of communication – communication is not an aspect of contract. Rather, contracts represent a particular way to communicate among other ways, with their own form and logic.

Second, contracts cannot be presumed to be legalised exchanges. As Macaulay has already shown, contracts do not necessarily have to be legal, although this requires a systematic abolition of the law as a privileged point of observation for contracts.

Third, partnerships should not be seen as something extra–contractual. Rather, we have to inquire more specifically into the way in which the form of contract is put under pressure and how that specifically displaces the contract's character of communicative form.

This chapter includes a form analysis of contracts and provides the basis for the analysis in the next chapter of the specific partnership form of contracts. The analysis is based primarily on the works of Niklas Luhmann and Gunther Teubner, but is also inspired by Jacques Derrida.

This chapter therefore has a presentation of how contracts are observable as a form of communication in a systems-theoretical sense. They are no longer objects that we look at, but particular distinctions that we can use to observe a particular kind of communication. Contracts come to comprise a particular communicative and expectation-forming perspective on the world. What does the world look like when observed through the lens of a contract? That is, how is the form 'contract' defined and how does that make possible and impossible respectively certain communicative formations of expectation? What we are looking for is the omnipresent communicative unity of contracts.

Form of contracts

Building on Niklas Luhmann, the proposition is to view contracts as a form of communication representing the unity of the difference of obligation and freedom. This form can be formalised as shown in Figure 5.1.

Figure 5.1: Form of contract

Obligation | Freedom

Contract

Luhmann proposes this view of a contract as the unity of obligation and freedom (Luhmann, 1981, p 249). A contract ties the freedom of the communication parties to obligation so that there is no obligation outside the freedom of the parties to limit their own freedom. But on the other hand, the freedom is also not freedom without its social realisation, that is, through tying the parties' realisation of freedom to each other in the form of obligations. Ownership, for example, can only be realised by entering into a relationship of obligation with someone else who then realises their freedom.

Contractual operations do indeed communicate about obligations but always presuppose the freedom of the contractual parties as the outside of the contract. Freedom is not indicated or spoken about in the communication, but is presupposed as a necessary basis for the formulation of reciprocally binding obligations. In the words of Durkheim: 'The only undertakings worthy of the name [contract] are those that are desired by individuals, whose sole origin is this free act of the will. Conversely, any obligation that has not been agreed by both sides is not in any way contractual' (Durkheim, 1984, p 158).

The traditional representation of a contract (which is also present in Macneil and Macaulay) is as an agreement about exchange between individual wills. Teubner, on the other hand, argues that modern contracts can hardly be viewed as such. He writes: 'Contract today can only be an interrelation between discourses' (Teubner, 2000, p 403). Contracts have to be viewed as an obligation between systems of communication rather than between individuals.

In order to function as a contract, they need an afterlife in which they are transformed by the related systems of communication. What constructs the contract as a contract is primarily the communication that results from it. It is the reception, the interpretation and generally the afterlife of the contract that makes a contract a contract. The afterlife of the contract consists of the fact that systems of communication continually establish internal orders in relation to their own interpretation of the contract.

However, if this is the case, it means that it is not possible for a contract to have only one meaning. First of all, the meaning behind the obligations has to be continuously recreated and, second, the meaning behind the obligations is established in different ways depending on the logic of the meaning-creating system of communication. This installs a basic paradox in the form of a contract, which Derrida formulates as: 'You are not responsible when you talk in the other's language' (Derrida, 1988, p 124).

Derrida goes on to write:

> You can only enter into a contract [...] if you do so in your own tongue. You're only responsible, in other words, for what you say in your own mother tongue. If, however, you say it only in your own tongue, then you're still not committed, because you must also say it in the other's language. An agreement or obligation of whatever sort – a promise, a marriage, a sacred alliance – can only take place, I would say, in translation, that is, only if it is simultaneously uttered in both my tongue and the other's. If it takes place in only one tongue, whether it be mine or the other's, there is no contract possible.[...] In order for the contract or the alliance to take place, in order for the 'yes, yes' to take place on both sides, it must occur in two languages at once.[...] Thus, the agreement, the contract in general, has to imply the difference of languages rather than transparent translatability, a Babelian situation which is at the same time lessened and left intact. If one can translate purely and simply, there is no agreement. And if one can't translate at all, there is no agreement either. In order for there to be an agreement, there has to be a Babelian situation, so that what I would call the translation contract – in the transcendental sense of this term, let's say – is the contract itself. Every contract must be a translation contract. There is no contract possible – no social contract possible – without a translation contract, bringing with it the paradox I have just mentioned. (Derrida, 1988, p 125)

In terms of systems theory, this means that a contract is always a contract between different systems of communication that remain operatively closed to one another. As operatively closed systems, they bring meaning to the contract in their own way. However, the way in which one system articulates the contract as something meaningful has to also make sense to the other systems. It has to be recognisable as obligation.

The paradox, in other words, is that a contract has to necessarily be one and also many at the same time. The contract between systems of communication has to simultaneously be a joined contract and an individual contract. Contracts are only able to maintain their unity by also being a plurality (see Figure 5.2).

Figure 5.2: The multiplicity of the contract

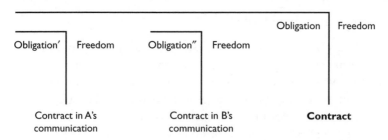

This means that a contract is not an independent system of communication but rather a coupling between different systems of communication. A contract has to presuppose the freedom of the systems of communication as the outside of obligation, but obligation cannot mean the same to the different systems of communication since every system has its own boundary of meaning and has to therefore define obligation within its communication in its own way. At the same time, however, obligation has to also mean the same, because otherwise there would be no connection. Teubner sums it as: 'The unity of contract today is fractured in the endless play of discourses. It sounds paradoxical, but one contract is in reality broken into a multiplicity of contracts' (Teubner, 2000, p 403).

What creates the contractuality of the contract are the individual and mutually closed systems of communication by defining the contract as an active communicative event in their respective systems: 'In its capacity of promise, the translation is already an event and the most important signature of a contract' (Derrida, 1989, p 165).

Couplings are always only couplings in relation to mutually closed systems. Structural couplings between systems of communication presuppose systems differentiation. However, this difference between coupling and differentiation has to also be a part of the very form of the coupling. As a coupling, the contract is not something that exists in the space between systems; the contract has to be inside each system from where it both joins and separates the systems (Luhmann, 1992b, p 1433). Contracts create mutual irritation through obligation. They irritate the individual system of communication into a commitment to an internal translation of obligation and to letting it grow and create structures in the internal communication. Freedom, on the other hand, is not merely individual will. Freedom as the outside of irritation defines a necessary indifference to the translation of obligation in the other implicated systems. Contracts connect systems of communication by simultaneously committing the individual system to translating the contract and by allowing for freedom in translating. Without the freedom of the other in translating the contract, there can be no contractual obligation on the other's side (see Figure 5.3).

Figure 5.3: The contract as structural coupling

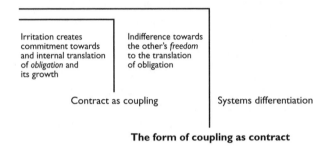

Irritation creates commitment towards and internal translation of *obligation* and its growth

Indifference towards the other's *freedom* to the translation of obligation

Contract as coupling

Systems differentiation

The form of coupling as contract

Thus, in this version, contract presupposes not only freedom of action as the other side of obligation but also freedom to translate obligation.

Contract and functional differentiation

If contracts represent couplings between social systems, the next question becomes how society is differentiated into different systems of communication.

In Chapter Three it was argued with reference to Luhmann that today's society is functionally differentiated, that is, society is divided into functional systems of communication that are closed around each of their functions, their medium of communication and their code. Thus, the economy, politics, law, love, religion, art and education represent different functional systems of communication. What follows are a few examples of functional communication in order to fully clarify the logic.

The legal system of communication: the law comprises a particular medium and a particular binary code. The symbolically generalised medium of the law is 'to apply' as in the expression 'applicable law'. The medium is symbolically recognised in the form of laws, clauses, legal decisions and regulations. The code is right/wrong, and it is naturally seen as better to be right than wrong. Thus, as symbolically generalised medium the law divides the world into right and wrong. Together, the code's two sides provide a complete description of the world. Right is always right in relation to wrong, and the distinction is not based in anything outside itself. Thus, the very establishment of the legal code means the exclusion of morality from the law. In legal communication, right is right and has nothing to do with justice. This also means that legal communication is paradoxically based, which becomes clear when the law inquires into its own code. Is the distinction between right/wrong itself right or wrong? The binary code of law creates the certainty that if a person is right, they are sure to have the law on their side. Uncertainty about the law exists only in a form, which can in principle be dissolved with reference to decisions created within the legal system itself (Luhmann, 1989, p 64). Functionally, the legal system of communication is closed around the function of providing against conflicts and establishing stable expectations that may survive specific disappointments. This function is expressed in the fact that the basic value of the legal system is the desire for social order. The fact that legal communication is directed at conflicts does not mean that law solves conflicts. On the other hand, when the law observes conflicts, the legal communication transforms them into legal problems about right and wrong. This is all that law understands and all that it is able to consider. The function of handling conflicts, therefore, is a question of defining rules that enable the law to transfer conflicts into the law and to define them as legal. This excludes the original 'substance' of the conflict. Assigning rights to people is one of the law's most important tools for enabling the transformation of conflicts into legal problems. For example, without legal ownership of your house, a neighbour dispute cannot be taken to court, and if it is taken to court, everything is excluded but the relevant facts for the determination of right and wrong, and legal communication might even employ the distinction between right/wrong in considering what counts as legal, for example, which facts are legal facts (Luhmann, 1992b). The law simplifies conflicts and specifies precisely what is included in the conflict and disregards the rest if the rest cannot be formulated in legal terms. For example, personal motives and interests are irrelevant in conflicts about purchases if these cannot be discussed in legal terms as preconditions.

The educational system of communication: according to Luhmann, the general symbolic medium of communication of education is 'the child' (Luhmann, 1993e). While there is a particular history associated with the emergence of the distinction between child and adult, there has not always been such a distinction. There have been periods, for example, when children were merely perceived to be small adults (Ariés, 1982). The modern notion about the relationship between child and adult was formed in the 1700s and dissolves the idea that a child develops into what they are born as. Instead, the child comes to be seen as mouldable. What the child develops into is seen as dependent on the environment that moulds the child. It leads to what has become the traditional discussion about heredity and environment, which fundamentally is a discussion about the plasticity of the child: to what extent is upbringing and education able to implicate the fate and nature of the individual child? Seeing the child as mouldable establishes the conditions for educational communication in which you do not actually talk with the child but where the 'child' is represented as a symbol of a learning endeavour. The child becomes a symbol by means of which communication can take place. They represent the *medium* to be *formed* in educational communication. What the child is to be formed into depends on the educational programme. The formation can be about pliancy, morality, creativity, professional knowledge or something entirely different. The fact that the child as a medium is a *general* symbolic medium for communication means that there are no restrictions as to the kind of knowledge that can be imprinted into the medium. In principle, the child can be moulded to become anything – for example, a dictator, an artist or an environmentally conscious citizen. The fact that the medium is *symbolic* means that the child functions as the symbolic and recognisable expression of the medium, that is, what we can communicate about. However, it is a variable symbol that can be replaced by, for example, pupil, student or course participant (and which, therefore, is not reliant on biological age). Regardless of the symbol, we maintain the same distinction: child/adult = mouldable/moulded. The binary *code* that the child is the bearer of is better/worse with respect to learning (Luhmann, 1989, pp 100-6). In educational communication, everything is observed from this perspective. Everything is observed with a view to perfecting. Thus, it is a *code of correction* by which you might either link up with the code's positive preference value, for example, by considering how the child/pupil/student/course participant may improve, or with the code's reflexive side by discussing why there is no improvement even with the employment of the most current educational methods. Naturally, the code is also employed in ongoing evaluations and tests of the child's competencies: passed/failed, strong/weak sides, and so on. At any rate, educational communication becomes a question of correction with a view to perfection.

The care system: in the system of care, the symbolically generalised medium is care, and the code is help/no help. When a client appeals to the care system, the system might place the appeal on either the help or no help side of the code. Only the care system can judge whether there is a need for help or not, and the precondition for this is a diagnosis of the problem. This also means that the reservoir of possible diagnoses in the care system determines the production of a need for help. And naturally the definition of a diagnosis is an internal element of the care system. From the perspective of the care system, problems in the external environment are indefinite until the care system has established a diagnosis, that is, has decided whether and in what way there is a need for help. Problems presented by a client in the system's environment, for example, to a social worker, are considered indefinite needs for help. Action cannot be taken on the basis of indefinite needs for help. Through internal diagnosing the system's communication, the indefinite need for help may be transformed into a definite need for help or a definite non-need for help. On this basis, the care system can then intervene methodically (Moe, 1998; la Cour, 2002). Thus, problems do not exist in advance as care problems in the system's environment. The system itself produces the problems that it responds to, and the capacity for problem production depends on the possibility of making diagnoses. Moreover, the care system may increase its capacity for communicative reflection by re-entering the code help/no help into itself. This enables the care system to communicate about forms of help as non-help. Hence the system can decide not to act in relation to a diagnosed need for help if it finds that over time the help will only further cement the client's role as client. Thus, the care system may vary and differentiate its internal operations indefinitely into distinctions such as help non-help, and help/help doing self-help.

The political system: in the political system, the symbolically generalised medium is power. The code of power is power superiority/power inferiority, which in democracies is divided into govern/governed and government/opposition. Power is often confused with coercion, but as a medium for communication power represents precisely the absence of coercion. Power and coercion are two different and mutually exclusive forms of communication. Coercion means to force someone into a specific line of action and presupposes a very physically present, precise and direct action in relation to the person who is forced to act.

The advantage of the modern medium of power is that it is able to transfer complexity from the one holding power superiority onto the power inferior, who has to carry and handle this complexity through ongoing interpretation of the intentions of the power superior. One example might be if the Ministry of Science required universities to develop education in communication without further specifying the idea behind the requirement. This not only puts a specific task on the universities but also the task of defining the task, and in their particular definition, the universities have to continually consider what could have been the Ministry's intention and realise the task on the basis of such considerations, knowing that they could never be certain about the intentions of the superior. More than likely, the reality is that there was no clear intention and that what the universities deliver, in addition to being a proposal for a new programme, also represents a suggestion of possible intent to the power superior who is always in a position to respond that the suggestion was not what they intended. Power is exercised when the power inferior feels uncertain about the power superior and regulates themselves on the basis of interpretations of the possible intentions of the power superior. Therefore, power presupposes the freedom of the power inferior. Power is to control the freedom of others. Thus, the greater the capacity for self-regulation in the inferior, the greater the overall potential for power. Coercion represents the outside of power. Power is non-coercion. Coercion is always present in the political system of communication as an alternative to power in the form of sanctions; however, as soon as the power superior decides to employ sanctions, the transferred complexity shifts back onto the power superior who then has to suddenly show their intentions. In the political system of communication, everything is potentially political, and the political system determines what is considered political and non-political respectively. And once the system places a theme on the politic side of the distinction, it is almost impossible for the system not to act on it. It is difficult to both politicise a theme and desist from political action (Luhmann, 1990c).

Table 5.1 is an attempt to summarise the most important modern function systems. In this way, today's society is differentiated into a range of function systems, each with their own symbolically generalised medium and each their own binary code or logic. This makes communication between function systems impossible. They are not placed in a hierarchical structure and there is no centre that is able to represent society as a whole. The function systems each have their own values, and these values, or codes, represent the blind spots

Table 5.1: Society's function systems

Function system	Medium	Code (+/−)	Function
Political system	Power	Govern/governed	Facilitates collectively binding decisions
System of science	Knowledge	True/false	Seek new knowledge
Economic system	Money	Have/not have	Scarcity management
Educational system	The child	Better/worse educationally	CV sorting
System of mass media	Information	Information/non-information	Produce irritation
Legal system	Law	Right/wrong	Take measures against conflict formation
Moral communication	None	Respect/disrespect	Increase conflicts
Art system	The work of art	Art/not art	Observation of the world
Healthcare system	Treatment	Healthy/ill	Prevent death
Care system	Care	Help/no help	Inclusion
Intimate communication	Love	Loved/not loved	Address the outmost personal
System of religion	Faith	Immanence/transcendence	Rule out contingency

of the systems that allow them to throw themselves into the future with highly limited resonance capacity.

On the other hand, the function systems are able to observe each other from within their individual horizons of meaning, but the different horizons of meaning cannot be joined to form a whole. There simply is no one place of privilege from which it can be determined whether law is better than help or money better than love. They are immune to each other's argumentation. The functions are operatively closed, but in turn cognitively open through observation. The way in which they observe each other is illustrated in Table 5.2 opposite (see Andersen and Born, 2003). Not all function systems have been included, but it is hoped that the five chosen will suffice to enable the reader to continue the line of thinking. As Table 5.2 shows, the code in which communication takes place determines the theme that is constructed. The reason that a blank field has been left in the place where a particularly coded communication observes itself is not that

Table 5.2: Poly-contextuality presented as a matrix of observation

	Law observed	Love	Economy	Mass media	Education
Law as observer	–	Love can be observed as a disruptive element and occasionally as a specific legal fact: a motive	Economy can be observed as legal fact in relation to the assessment of motives and permeates the notion of subject	Mass media are observed as public control but also as a risk for the derailment of legal communication and of the possibility of a fair verdict	Education can be observed in the capacity of legal recognition of formal qualifications
Love	Love can observe the law as its ultimate opposite	–	Economy can be observed as the boundary of anticipation	Mass media can be observed as a space in which one may declare one's love in front of others	Education can be observed as a specific forming of love
Economy	Economy can observe law as a supplier of transaction forms and as punishment as the price for particular behaviour	Love can be observed as an article that can be bought	–	Mass media are observable as a space in which one can follow the development of the markets	Education is observable as priced competencies and can thus be transformed into a scarce resource
Mass media	The law can be observed as a particular journalistic genre	Love is observable as a particular journalistic genre	Economy is observable as a particular journalistic genre	–	Education can be observed as a particular journalistic genre
Education	The law is observable as a necessary but problematic evaluation unit for learning	Love can be observed as the precondition of engaged learning	Economy can be observed as an obstacle to learning	Mass media can be observed as a specific social educational medium	–

it could not be filled in but that it entails a comprehensive isolated question about self-reference and paradox, which has been left out. In brief, this question concerns the fact that the law, for example, when observing the law faces the paradoxical question about whether the code right/wrong is itself right or wrong.

We can describe the relationship between contract and society as follows: society is, on the one hand, functionally differentiated into a range of systems of communication, communicating in their own medium and code and hence operatively closed to each other. On the other hand, contract and society are able to observe each other, and systems couplings strengthen these reciprocal observations. Contracts represent such a coupling. There are other kinds of couplings, primarily organisations, but also themes produced by the mass media. Thus, we can illustrate the relationship between contract and society as shown in Figure 5.4.

Figure 5.4: Contract versus functional differentiation

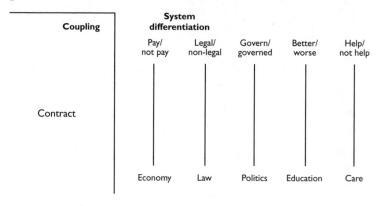

If contracts can indeed function as couplings between different function systems, it means that the individual functional systems of communication in their own communication can create contracts as a meaningful element. Basically, it is a question of how contracts are observable from inherently different communicative codes. If we try to observe this, we realise that the multiplicity of obligation in the different contract-reading systems is not a simple question of precision or weighting. A contract is constructed as radically different in the framework of different systems' observations of it (Teubner, 2000).

However, in a historical perspective contracts are *not* created to join all types of function systems. If we begin by looking at traditional contracts, those contracts that Macneil refers to as transactional or discrete are characterised by a relatively simple content and short time frame. These contracts are only observable as a legal promise and economic exchange respectively, and from a legal point of view an exchange is always the exchange of promises. From an evolutionary perspective, the classic contract is designed primarily to create a coupling between law and economy and as such is, among other things, the precondition of company differentiation (Luhmann, 1992a, pp 1435-6, 2004, pp 395-6; Teubner, 1992). For that reason, it is primarily jurisprudence and economic science that have developed a more sophisticated semantic in relation to contracts, whereas the concept of a contract plays only a marginal role in, for example, political science and sociology. As a coupling between law and economy the contract must be readable and translatable in a unique legal and economic way.

The legal system communicates through the code of right/wrong. From this perspective, a contract represents a promise and as such it enables the law to consider a conflict over an agreement and assess who is right and who is wrong in the conflict. Legal communication is closed around the function of providing against conflict development and it is in this light that the writing of a formal contract is seen.

The economic system communicates through the code to pay/not pay and from this perspective the contract represents not a promise but an exchange programme that conditions payments. Entering a contractual agreement means to arrive at the right price in a continual oscillation between the passive form of the code, to have/not have, and its active form, to pay/not pay. It is better to have than not to have, but to pay distributes both solvency and insolvency, and to buy something prevents someone from buying something else.

At the same time as law and economy are both able to give internal meaning to the contract, they can also give meaning to each other's interpretations of the contract. Thus, the law may understand exchange as the exchange of a promise and economy may understand a promise as a transaction cost (see Table 5.3).

Table 5.3: The contract's traditional coupling of law and economy

System of communication	Code	Contract translation	Observation of each other's observations of contracts
Legal system	Right/wrong	Promise	Exchange as the exchange of promises
Economic system	Pay/not pay	Exchange	Promises as transaction costs

In summary:

- Contracts represent a specific form of communication.
- The form of contract is the unity of obligation and freedom, that is, any contractual formulation of obligations presupposes the freedom of the participants to commit their freedom.
- Contracts are not established primarily between individuals but between systems of communication.
- In order for the contract to be given an afterlife as self-commitment in the individual system this means that freedom as the unmarked outside of contract is primarily a freedom of translation for the individual system of communication to assign meaning to the contractual obligation on their own communicative terms.
- Thus, any contract is a multiplicity and as such obtains the character of structural coupling.
- As a structural coupling a contract is not something in between but a simultaneity in which the implicated systems, each in their own way, construct the contract as an internal communicative element, for example, in law as a promise and in economy as an exchange.

SIX

Partnerships as second-order contracts

The concept of partnership is symptomatic of current new expectations that are put on contracts as form. As illustrated in the introduction to this book, a contract is put under pressure when it is set in the context of cross-sectoral collaboration, collectivity, agreements under developing conditions, project orientation and a focus on the future and visions. A contract is put under pressure when it is no longer perceived as functional in relation to conflict management, as we saw in the case of ISS Catering (pp 55-67). Moreover, a contract is put under pressure when it is seen as the counterconcept of partnerships. And finally, a contract is put under pressure when jurisprudence looks for ways to abolish the boundary between public and private and incorporate extra-contractual elements about justice into the contract.

We are left with two possibilities for the further analysis of partnerships. We can either subscribe to the contrasting of partnership and contract inherent in the partnership semantic and subsequently try to develop a theory about partnerships as a communicative form radically different from a contract as form. Or we can choose to see a partnership as a particular form of contract. It is the latter possibility that is pursued here. Thus, it is argued that the difference between partnership and contract is located within the form of contract, that the difference between contract and partnership is not essential and that partnership is a functional displacement of contract – a displacement, which, as will become apparent, has a number of implications.

What it is hoped to observe is a displacement in the form of contract and hence also a displacement in the way in which structural couplings are established between function systems. We will study partnerships as folded into a contract, a fold that is far from innocuous because it changes more than a few contractual properties. A partnership represents not merely a variation but a dislocation of the inner logic of a contract. Therefore, it is suggested that we see partnerships not as a radical new phenomenon but as an internal form displacement of an old form. As we saw in the previous chapter, a contract as a form contains a number of inherent tensions and paradoxes. Now, we will look at what happens to these in the partnership folding of a contract.

Partnerships need to be understood as second-order contracts. They are about committing to a future commitment, and this is what the partnership semantics entails when it says that we first have to choose each other and subsequently make agreements. The relationship can be illustrated as shown in Figure 6.1.

Figure 6.1: Partnerships as second-order contracts

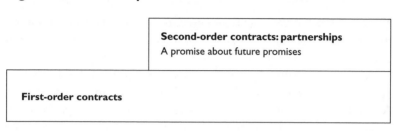

Partnerships are contracts about the fact *that* the parties agree to enter into contractual agreements with each other in the future, about *how* the parties plan to make contractual agreements in the future, and about how the parties will *relate to* the agreed first-order contracts. All three aspects are important and will be further explained in the following sections of this chapter; however, we will begin with a few preliminary thoughts.

Partnerships define a commitment to accept future commitments to the extent that they define the overall purpose of the collaboration. The overall purposes, as indicated, for example, in the Hørsholm Hospital partnership, do not represent operationalised goals. Rather, they are goals about goals, about outlining an image of the future and a general vision for the hospital. In that sense, they are a commitment towards future commitments.

Partnerships also define how the parties will form contracts in the future, for example, by defining a common management group responsible for representing the partnership. The management group is not anything in itself. It does not manage anything but the process in which new common projects are launched and agreed on.

Finally, partnerships are about defining and regulating that place from which first-order contracts are read. Defining values and missions in a partnership is more than empty rhetoric. It is a question of creating commitment towards a way of reading the first-order contracts so that they are not simply read from the perspective of the individual interests of either the provider or the customer but from an agreed definition of a common interest. It is a question of defining rules for interpretation that suspend legal disputes in the case of uncertainty about the interpretation of first-order contracts. It is also a question of making contracts about how to deal with incomplete contracts, contracts about not exploiting incomplete contracts for people's own short-term benefit.

Partnerships, therefore, are not about *being* more collective, mutual, dialogical, and so on than in the case of regular contracts. What is referred to by 'collective' or 'dialogue' are second-order agreements. It is not a form of merging or communitarianistic fusions of organisations. 'Collective' is merely a contractual term for a second-order commitment.

Whereas first-order contracts concern promises, second-order contracts represent a promise about promises. And a promise about a promise is of a radically different social quality than a promise. A first-order contract presupposes a social order of, for example, legal character. Besides the contract itself, a promise in a first-order contract refers to the law as an installation of order. This is what is so apparent in the works of Macneil and Macaulay; the law is always presupposed as the neutral ground on which contracts are formed. By contrast it is argued that partnerships represent an emergent social order. A promise about a promise does not presuppose an existing order but creates its own order. First-order contracts make external reference to an externally defined legal order. Partnerships are self-referential and create their own order. This is what the second-order promise is about: to create preconditions and premises for future promises. If this is true, it can be seen in the way in which partnerships define their own communicative structures in the form of time, factuality and sociality. A step-by-step illustration of this process is presented below.

Partnerships stabilise expectations under the expectation of changing expectations. If we observe partnerships in terms of communication theory as contracts it becomes clear that time is defined differently in partnerships than in traditional transactional contracts, something that Macneil and Macaulay also observed but did not think through.

The first consideration here is that partnerships provide an answer to a particular problem that has occurred in relation to the fact that organisations today define their internal time differently than previously. In the public sector the concept of time has been fundamentally displaced over the past 25 years, and a similar development can be seen in the private and voluntary sector. Using the public sector as a point of observation, this shift can be described as follows.

During the planning semantics in the public sector in the 1960s and 1970s (Andersen, 1995), change was perceived fundamentally differently than today. The central concepts then were reforms and adaptive measures. Public management during the 1960s and 1970s meant to identify specific developments in the environment and to prescribe reforms that could adjust the administration and policies to the new conditions. There was a prevalent conception that the world was moving in one particular direction and that you had to adapt to this direction of movement. It was typically thought that by analysing history you could make projections that could then work as the basis for decisions. Thus, change was always change on the basis of stability. Stability was the condition for learning, analysing your own development and specifying elements that needed to be reformed. The relationship between a temporal dimension and a factual dimension in the semantic was defined in a way so that the factual dimension was given priority. The precondition of change was factual analysis of history and the environment. It was problem-driven, with incremental changes (see Figure 6.2).

Figure 6.2: Time in the planning semantics

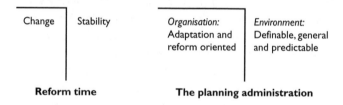

From the 1980s onwards, a new semantics emerged relating to administrative policy concerning the public sector. It is often referred to as 'new public management'. The notion of time in this semantics was radically different. The environment and its development was not described simply as definite as, for example, 'this is how the development is'. The environment was described as indefinite. It is often said that 'the world is increasingly complex', 'change is here to stay' and 'the world is a turbulent place'. The posed challenge becomes how to adapt to an increasingly complex, turbulent and continually changing environment. If the world is indeed more complex than what we can specifically describe and hence has to be indicated indefinitely as 'complex', how may an organisation counterbalance this fact? The answer today is adaptation and flexibility. We are no longer expected to adapt to anything specific; we are expected to adapt to the unknown. We might refer to it as adapting to adaptation. It is a question of having the ability to constantly be something different than what you are, not reforming yourself – reform means to move in a specific direction. Modern change management is something else; it is about maintaining the ability to change direction. Change no longer happens on the basis of stability since the only stable element is constant change and turbulence. Thus, the public sector makes a shift from perceiving change as a movement towards specific goals, a movement based on stability and ultimately resulting in new stability, to perceiving change as a pulse. It is not change with a defined and definite goal. It is not change in relation to something else. It is change or non-change (Andersen and Born, 2000). It is change with a view to more change. This also upsets the balance between the factual dimension and the temporal dimension in the semantics so that the temporal dimension has priority. Instead of problem-driven change, we get change-driven factuality (see Figure 6.3).

Figure 6.3: Time in the semantics of new public management

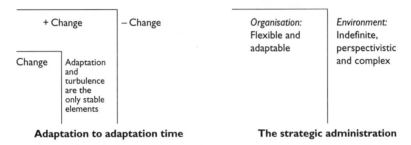

With organisations seeking to maximise the capacity to be something else, the individual organisation becomes a reference point for a range of adaptation projects that do not necessarily pull the organisation in the same direction. The individual organisation works strategically with many different totalities and many future scenarios that are not necessarily mutually coherent.

A similar trend can be observed in the private sector. Moreover, the private sector is becoming increasingly dependent on its agreements with the public sector and it is for this reason alone tied to the constructions of the public sector. Subscribing to the diagnosis of current organisations as working under the notion of having to adapt and prepare for the unknown leads to at least one challenge about how to make ties with organisations in your environment without causing them to impede your own adaptability. The reason that the public sector in the 1980s was so eager to transfer responsibilities onto private and voluntary organisations was primarily the effort to increase its adaptability (Andersen, 1997). Outsourcing became linked to the notion of focusing efforts around strategic responsibilities and entrusting the management of responsibilities to operating units. Different operators can compete for the best solutions. It is easy to increase or decrease activities, for example. However, when entering a long-term contract with a private provider about a complex service such as train services, payroll systems or nursing homes, you run the risk of reducing the desired adaptability due to the long-term conditions of the agreement. As Campbell and Harris express it: 'The problem is that presentation is a quite illusory goal and all long-term contracts must in practice be incomplete' (1993, p 169). The consequence is that 'contracts had all been transformed into more flexible forms, with prices, quantities, and delivery dates becoming open to subsequent determination' (1993, p 172).

In this context, partnerships can be seen as an attempt to find an equivalent answer to the problem of committing in the long term without losing adaptability. However, in order for that to be possible, partnerships need to have a different inherent concept of time than traditional contracts. What that means is a division of the temporal dimension into one temporality for first-order contracts and a different temporality for second-order contracts, where second-order contracts have to incorporate the contract's temporal plasticity (see Figure 6.4).

Figure 6.4: The first- and second-order temporal dimension

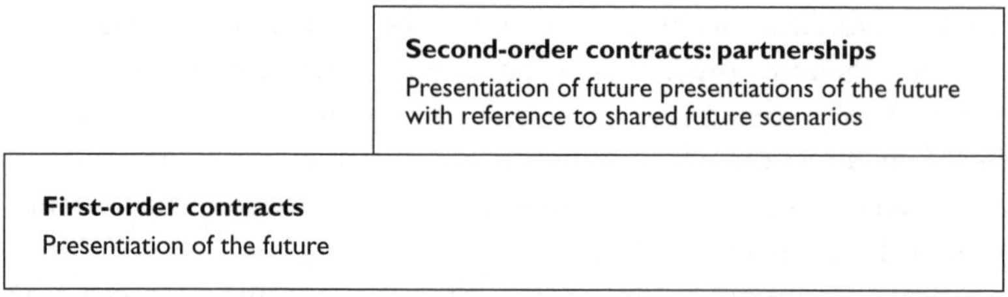

Second-order contracts: partnerships
Presentation of future presentiations of the future with reference to shared future scenarios

First-order contracts
Presentiation of the future

In a certain sense, time becomes the issue. First-order contracts focus on exchange. The issue is what is to be exchanged, for example, money for building maintenance. In contrast, second-order contracts focus on development. What is exchanged are promises about promises, including promises about self-development with a view to common development. Second-order contracts are about joint projects for development, for example, which hospital is to be developed in the future, which highway to be built around a city or how to extend collaboration. Thus, what defines the development are expectations about the future. It becomes crucial in partnerships to formulate horizons for the future. In the temporal dimension in first-order contracts, a contract represents a presentation of the future. A first-order contract has to specify in the present what is to be exchanged in the future. A second-order contract, on the other hand, has to indicate a horizon in the present for how the parties will work to specify new possible exchanges in the future. Here, horizons for the future do not represent a promise about specific actions in the future. Horizons for the future are also not prognoses for particular developments of needs in order to plan for services. Horizons for the future represent images of what the collaboration might consist of in the future, including entirely new responsibilities and visions. They are expectations of future expectations of the collaboration. A promise about horizons for the future and visions is a promise about a premise for a subsequent promise, which should be seen in the context of the previously stated argument about partnerships as a form of contract that creates its own internal structures and order.

Thus, second-order contracts concern a stabilisation of expectations under the expectation of changing expectations.

Partnerships define factual perspectives for the creation of facts

This form of organisation of the temporality of partnerships has a number of implications for the factual dimension of contracts. First-order contracts are about concrete exchange, and on the factual dimension this concerns the specification of what is to be exchanged, that is, for example, the description of the building maintenance that is expected in return for a specific sum of money. Second-order contracts, on the other hand, grant priority to the temporal dimension because what is to be exchanged are possibilities for development. The facts cannot be specified because they do not yet exist. The facts of the collaboration depend on the specifics of the future development. Factuality appears in partnerships as suspended, as the result of a development (see Figure 6.5).

Let us look at the formulation of the tender terms and conditions and the subsequent partnership contract in connection with Hørsholm Hospital. The tender terms and conditions emphasise the overall vision for the hospital:

> 'the vision for Hørsholm Hospital is to work as the patients' hospital, offering the best treatment in the country. The vision, therefore, is to create the best hospital in Denmark. The hospital emphasises values such as strong professional quality

Figure 6.5: The first- and second-order factual dimension

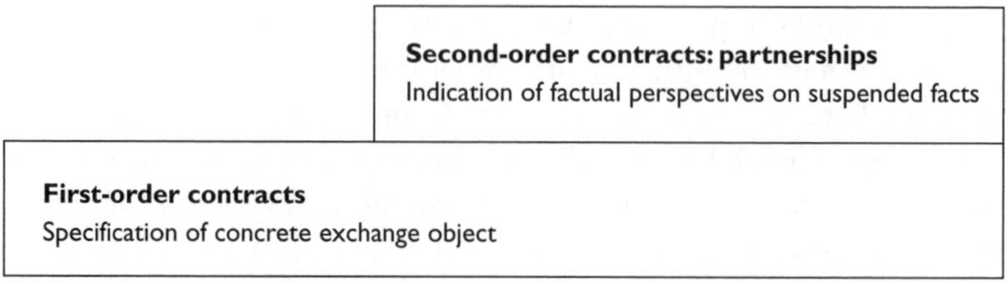

Second-order contracts: partnerships Indication of factual perspectives on suspended facts

First-order contracts Specification of concrete exchange object

and expertise, an optimal service for patients and relatives, minimal waiting time and strong financial performance. Therefore, Hørsholm Hospital focuses all resources on carrying out all operations and treatments within the hospital's fields of expertise. It focuses on a service-driven operation based on efficient planning of patient care and an integrated approach to services that the individual patient/user experiences in their contact with the hospital' (Hørsholm Hospital, 2001a, pp 3-4). The vision hardly addresses the specific case but only the factual approaches to the case. To simply emphasise 'vision' is an indication that the object of exchange is something that is to be developed and improved in the process. Statements like 'the patients' hospital', 'service-driven operation' and 'integrated approach' simply indicate factual perspectives on the development.

Naturally, tender material contains more than a vision. It also contains a description of the services. However, even here we find a second-order perspective. About the performance catalogue it says: 'Appendix 1 does not primarily describe *how* to solve the advertised services, but rather *which* types of responsibilities to solve, and *which output* is expected from these. Since the partnership agreement is based on a mutual desire to develop new ways and models for handling the specific service responsibilities, the tender material invites the tenderer to provide suggestions and ideas for solving the task and possibilities for future solutions to the extent that this is possible' (Hørsholm Hospital, 2001a, p 5). Notice that the text writes *types* of responsibilities. It is not only a question of not having determined a method. The responsibilities are not clearly defined but are expected to be defined later in the process.

You might expect that the final contract would clearly and unambiguously specify the services, but even that is not the case. Even here, the emphasis is on the description of the perspective rather than on the facts. The performance catalogue in the contract says: 'It has been a conscious decision to only include limited details in the descriptions' (Hørsholm Hospital, 2001b, p 5). Instead, the descriptions primarily address perspectives and considerations. About general requirements in relation to the responsibilities, it says: 'Implicit in what Hørsholm Hospital expects of its partner is the continual fulfillment of the following requirements: the working environment must not deteriorate in relation to the current level. When possible, consideration has to be given to environmentally sound and energy saving purchases. When working for Hørsholm Hospital, the partner's employees have to wear the same uniform as the rest of the hospital's employees' (Hørsholm Hospital, 2001b, p 5). It seems odd to explicitly indicate the expectations as 'implicit', but it probably means that these expectations about factual perspectives should not have to be discussed in the future. They are expected to be met automatically.

In the description of the sub-tasks, emphasis is also on the perspective of the tasks. The description of each sub-task includes a section called non-negotiable requirements that specifically define the perspective requirements. For example, in relation to the sub-task of food production and delivery to patients, the non-negotiable requirements are:

> There must be a reasonable possibility for choice of menu and choice between different types of food (full diet, super diet, vegetarian diet and non-pork diets), and types of diet.[...] In cooperation with the hospital it is the responsibilities of the partners to ensure an ongoing adjustment of the selection of foods in relation to new patient groups, composition of population, and other gradual changes in food requirements.[...] The food must continually meet current recommendations for Danish institutional food and the dietary policies of Frederiksborg county.[...] A certain share of products used in the production of food must be organic. (Hørsholm Hospital, 2001b, p 9, part 3)

Partnerships determine their own partnership subjects

Finally, partnerships are radically different from first-order contracts in relation to the social dimension. As mentioned earlier, first-order contracts presuppose the contractual parties as independent actors with independent rights. This means that the central focus in contract communication is on mutual obligations but with the continuous precondition that the participants remain free to limit their own freedom. With partnerships, however, this is not as obvious.

Even in complex first-order contracts that focus on goals but provide freedom of method to its providers, we see a strong interest in the contracting party. Is the general contractor technically and organisationally capable of keeping their promises when the agreement concerns the construction of a particular well-defined part of a road? Is the company capable of building the road? The formation of a first-order contract often entails requirements about documenting the capacity of the builder. However, capacity, meaning the contracting party's preconditions as contracting party, is still presupposed. It is seen as a condition outside the contract that can be assessed or not assessed, documented or not documented.

This is different in partnerships. A central focus in partnerships in their capacity of a promise about subsequent promises becomes the partners' self-creation as relevant partnership partners. The freedom of the partner as relevant partner is no longer presupposed. What partnerships seek to establish is precisely the partner's freedom to commit to assuming responsibility for the partnership. Partnerships represent an attempt to formulate mutual obligations concerning the self-creation of individual partners as responsible for and relevant to the partnership. It concerns the obligation to create yourself as a free and independent partner for the partnership – obligation towards freedom in the image of the partnership. Thus, the partnership form becomes rather complex. It requires freedom reintroduced as obligation, but at the same time it has to presuppose freedom since otherwise there could be no obligation towards freedom (see Figure 6.6).

Figure 6.6: The social dimension on the first and second order

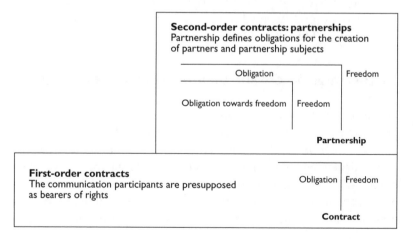

Here is a concrete example of this partnership form. The example pertains to a partnership about the capacity building of farmers in Bangladesh who do not own land. This project is chosen because Danida chose to emphasise the project as exemplary (Projektrådgivningen, 2006). It was also chosen because of the extent to which it focuses on the creation of the partner. The example is rather sophisticated: through the Danish embassy in Bangladesh and the Danish NGO Danmission, Danida finances an NGO in Bangladesh. This NGO would not even exist without the initial Danish financial support and is established in order to provide Danmission and others with a partner for a particular project. The NGO is called SUPOTH (Scheme for Underprivileged People to Organise Themselves) and its board consists primarily of members of the Lutheran Church in Bangladesh. The partnership is called the SUPOTH project and besides SUPOTH its partners are Danmission and the development department of the Danish Missionary Council. The purpose of the partnership is to increase the population's income and employment opportunities combined with an effort to increase literacy, raise awareness of oppression of women in particular and environmental, nutritional and health issues. The goals are not to be pursued directly but instead through the establishment of self-help groups in the villages. Self-help groups are organised locally. In 2002 this amounted to 331 groups with a total of 6,000 members. Each group elects representatives for so-called unions, which consist of 8–10 groups. The unions elect representatives for regional Thana associations, of which there were approximately 40 in 2002. The SUPOTH project instructs, trains and supports the individual Thana associations. The objective of the training and support is to establish the individual Thana as free and independent in relation to the project. Thus, the partnership project is a question of creating Thana associations as self-creating partners, capable of locally generating additional partners in the form of groups and unions. A monitoring tool has been developed to steer the process, consisting of five community capacity indicators (CCIs): (1) group financial capacity, (2) group management capacity, (3) group technical capacity, (4) networking capacity and (5) social control capacity. These indicators are used to monitor and instruct the Thanas: once a Thana association has achieved all five capacities, it is considered an independent local partner, capable of being in charge of and assuming the role of the SUPOTH project. Moreover, this creation of the function of self-creation in the partnership is twofold in the sense that the individual Thana associations are assigned the same function of capacity building in relation to local groups, which are then instructed and supported by Thana on the basis of the five indicators. Once a local group has gone through the capacity building process, it becomes independent from the SUPOTH project, and this process is referred to as graduation. In 2002 a total of 80 groups graduated. The project estimates that it takes a group five years from when it is established until it becomes independent and graduates. NGO consultant Troels Hovgaard summarises the experiences from the project as: 'Empowerment is achieved on the basis of an improved economic situation for the individual person and of the acquisition of new skills (eg reading and writing abilities), but perhaps most significantly from an experience of being in control of your own and the common development, achieved through capacity building in planning, management, collaboration, and project management' (Hovgaard, 2002, p 1). It is clear that the partnership does not presuppose its partners. The objective is to create the partners according to a specific partner concept. Committing to being part of the SUPOTH project means a commitment to creating yourself as a free partner.

Conclusion

When we choose to observe partnerships as a form of contract they emerge as second-order contracts. Whereas a contract can be seen as a promise, partnerships become a promise about promises. Partnerships become a second-order promise, which affects the contractual definition of time, factuality and sociality.

On the temporal dimension, a contract can be seen as the presentation of the future. Partnerships as second-order contracts concern the presentation of the future presentation of the future. On the factual dimension, a first-order contract represents a specification of the specific exchange object. On the second-order level of a partnership, a contract becomes the indication of factual perspectives on suspended facts, that is, facts about facts. Finally, on the social dimension a first-order contract can be seen as an exchange of commitment between the contractual parties whose status as holders of rights is presupposed. With partnerships as second-order contracts this cannot be presupposed because partnerships are precisely about the creation of partnership-relevant partners.

This shift from first-order to second-order contracts is an expression of more than simply a more or less random historical variation of the phenomenon of contract. When contracts 'turn second order' this is due to the recognition in organisations of the fact that the preconditions of first-order contracts are slipping – on the factual, temporal as well as social dimension. The level of complexity pertaining to the facts changes: the object of exchange is no longer given. The level of complexity pertaining to time changes: the object of the promise is constantly changing and cannot be stabilised. The level of complexity pertaining to the social changes: the definition of relevant partners has become fluid and diverse and something to be established in the process.

Thus, partnerships have to be seen as functionally equivalent to contracts under conditions where the preconditions for first-order contracts disintegrate. Partnerships represent a functionally equivalent response to disintegrating preconditions. They stabilise expectations with the expectation of changing preconditions. Partnerships describe factual perspectives on not yet established facts and create their own relevant partners.

Perhaps we can give an even more specific diagnosis; whereas the indefiniteness of the facts in a first-order contract, for example, can be seen as a form of dysfunctionality, this indefiniteness is precisely what makes the partnership work. Partnerships simply presuppose non-presupposed and non-defined preconditions. What is argued is that this shift from first-order to second-order contracts represents an extraordinarily radical displacement of the contract's form. Indeed, what characterises partnerships is that they are a self-creating form, which is in sharp contrast to first-order contracts. First-order contracts presuppose an existing order within which the contract can be established on all three meaning dimensions: time, fact and sociality. The partnership, on the other hand, is designed to create its own preconditions, including its own time, factuality and sociality. First-order contracts refer externally to conditions that precede the contract and are considered stable. Partnerships are self-referential and refer to conditions that they themselves establish and that are never perceived to be stable since a partnership only exists in its topical transformation. There is no partnership unless it is transformed into new first-order agreements, unless there is a continual production of new presentations of future presentations of the future. When entering into a first-order contract, you know that you have a contract, and when you have a contract, you become a contractual party whether or not the contract is breached, since a breach of contract also represents part of the afterlife of the contract. In a partnership, on the other hand, you cannot know until afterwards whether you were actually a partner because a partnership is precisely about partner creation. If in the end there is no afterlife to the partnership agreement, there is simply no partnership, not even a dissolved partnership, although there might be disappointed expectations. Thus, partnerships are not just second-order contracts;

they are also a second-order social order created to exist only in its making. Partnerships represent an emergent order, always in the making and never more than precisely in the making.

As formulated by Maas and Bakker in a somewhat different language:

> A multi-paradigmatic partnership cannot be understood by predefined rules or meanings.[...] In conclusion, it means that these kinds of partnerships ask for 'unfrozen circumstances' in which dynamic, social spaces and fluid forms can be examined as long as necessary. (Maas and Bakker, 2000, p 198; see also Callon, 1998, on 'hybrid forms')

Wittel speaks about how social contracts in the network society obtain a transitory character, where relations are not something you have, and not something you do, but something that is to be constantly used and hence produced and renewed (Wittel, 2001, pp 66, 72).

If this represents a fairly accurate diagnosis of the contractual form of a partnership, the next question is whether or not this has implications for the relationship between contract and society. The question is whether the shift from first-order to second-order contracts also displaces the contract's character of structural coupling between the function systems of society. Thus, it is suggested that partnerships not only change the contract form but also the mutual relations between the function systems of society. This is the focus of the next chapter.

SEVEN

Partnerships as tentative structural coupling

Partnerships have been discussed as a form of contract. Here, the studies are taken one step further and there is a discussion of whether the displacement of the form has consequences for a contract as a structural coupling between function systems. The argument is that partnerships not only presuppose the coupling of a greater number of function systems than traditional contracts, they also change the way in which couplings are established.

As mentioned in Chapter Five, a contract does not represent an independent system of communication but a coupling between different systems of communication. A contract has to presuppose the freedom of the systems of communication as outside obligation, but it cannot be the same obligation for different systems of communication, since each system has its own meaning boundary and has to therefore assign meaning to obligation in its communication in its own way. At the same time, however, the obligation has to be the same since there would otherwise be no connection. Teubner summarises it as follows: 'The unity of contract today is fractured in the endless play of discourses. It sounds paradoxical, but one contract is in reality broken into a multiplicity of contracts' (Teubner, 2000, p 403).

So which function systems are coupled with partnerships and with the possibility of constructing the partnership as an internal systemic commitment? Which form does this commitment take in different function systems? And which freedom and hence mutual indifference between function systems are defined with partnerships?

As mentioned in Chapter Five, the traditional contract couples the legal function system and the economic function system in that the form of contract allows for a simultaneous different construction of the contract in the two systems: as a promise in the legal perspective and as an exchange in the economic perspective. Moreover, law and the economy give meaning to each other's contractual constructions. The construction of contract as a promise in law can be seen in the economy as a transactional cost. The construction of a contract in the economy as an exchange can be seen in legal terms as an exchange of binding promises.

Many more complicated and flexible forms of contract expand the demands on a contract as structural coupling. This pertains, for example, to public outsourcing to private companies but also to long-term sub-supplier agreements between private companies. For example, when the state develops tender material for public welfare services such as home care, train services or hospital laboratory tasks, the contract must be able to have an afterlife in additional communication systems rather than simply law and the economy. From a legal point of view Campbell and Harris state: 'The form of long-term contracts as documents will tend to be open-ended and to display a rejection of the goal of presentation in favour of explicit flexibility [...] in addition to the explicit sophistication of these documents, there will be a co-operative recourse to extra-legal strategies to resolve problems which cannot be handled under the documents' (Campbell and Harris, 1993, p 174). This also demands, they say, that the parties to the contract will 'adopt a co-operative rather than narrowly maximizing, opportunistic attitude to their own and others' performance' (Campbell and Harris, 1993, p 174).

When outsourcing home care, the contract cannot only be read as an economic and legal commitment; it has to make political sense as the implementation of a particular policy and political decision. Moreover, it has to make sense within the care communication responsible for translating the contractual definition of services into practice. Several examples from the outsourcing of home care show that a contract far from always allows for a care-based reading. When services become specified in detail so that each home care operation is defined both in terms of content and duration, it means that the care communication is precluded from providing the contract with a meaningful afterlife; home care workers are no longer care givers but simply service workers. With an exact definition of the number of minutes allowed for helping with tooth brushing, shaving, hair washing, and so on, there is literally 'not much to talk about' in terms of care. Care becomes simplified into services (Højlund and Højlund, 2000; la Cour and Højlund, 2003; Højlund, 2004b).

In most outsourcings there are at least four different function systems involved in giving meaning to a contract in order to give the contract a communicative afterlife and hence function as an actual contract: the economic, legal and political systems and one (or more) service-related systems. These four systems will not be able to observe the contract in the same way; a contract becomes constructed in four radically different ways (Teubner, 1998, 2000). This is shown in Table 7.1.

We have already discussed law and the economy. The communicative code in the legal function system is right/wrong and legal

Table 7.1: Contractual construction in relation to outsourcing

System of communication	Code	Contractual construction
Legal system	Right/wrong	Promise
Economic system	Pay/not pay	Exchange
Political system	Govern/governed	Instrument for implementation
Service-related system	+/– performativity	Service programme

communication is concerned with taking measures against conflict formation.

In this perspective, a contract represents a promise where the specification of the promise can be part of a legal fallout in the determination of right and wrong in relation to the promise. Thus, a contract is designed with reference to the possibility of subsequently settling potential conflict between the contractual parties. The more specifically the promise is described, the better the chances of determining right and wrong in relation to the promise. In a legal perspective, a promise is simply a programme for the determination of right and wrong in a relation of private law between legal subjects.

In economic communication, however, a contract is something entirely different. The code of economic communication is to pay/ not to pay, and here a contract is a programme for future payments in connection with the exchange of services.

But in outsourcing, the political system of communication has to also be able to assign meaning to the contract in order for the contract to be given a political afterlife, for example, in the form of a political decision to hold the mayor responsible for failing to oversee the contract. The political system communicates through the code of govern/governed and can observe contracts as a way to realise and implement policies. When entering into an agreement with a private company about childcare or train services, the question is whether or not you obtain control through the contract. From a political perspective, the contract represents neither a promise nor an exchange, but primarily a form of governance where the goal is to maximise governance. This also means that a specific outsourcing project always has the possibility of choosing an alternative form of governance. In political terms, the contract is one governance technology among others.

Finally, outsourcing is essentially about services provided by one or more function systems. If the specific outsourcing project concerns hospital management, it becomes critical for the healthcare system to be able to assign meaning to the outsourcing as a health programme. If the outsourcing concerns a specific social treatment facility, the contract has to be able to be read on the basis of the code of the social care system, help/no help, in which communication is always a question of transforming indefinite needs for help into definite needs for help through diagnosing that leads to treatment and intervention. Thus perceived, a contract represents a treatment programme that provides certain possibilities for intervention on the basis of a specific diagnosis. If a contract is agreed on between ISS Junior Service and a municipality concerning three daycare institutions, the contract also has to be meaningful as a programme for pedagogical services. The point should be clear: an outsourcing contract represents a coupling between different systems and can *only* work as such if the different systems are able to simultaneously construct an internal definition of a given contract and to remain selectively indifferent to the different contractual constructions of other systems.

If we install once again the distinction between first-order and second-order contracts, we are able to specify the possibilities of the different function systems to assign meaning to contracts. Indeed, the conditions for assigning meaning to a contract are very different in the two orders and implicate, therefore, the function systems and their mutual relations (see Table 7.2).

Table 7.2: Contractual construction in relation to partnerships

System of communication	Code	First-order contract	Second-order contract
Legal system	Right/wrong	Promise about action	Promise about promises
Economic system	To pay/not pay	Exchange	Exchange of possibilities for exchange
Political system	Govern/ governed	Instrument of implementation	Constitution: decision about decision
Service-related system	+/− performativity	Service programme	Programme for service programming

Partnerships as a political constitution

When the *political system* observes outsourcing contracts it sees a tool for governance and implementation with particular benefits and disadvantages in relation to other tools. One of the most mentioned benefits of outsourcing is that it means that the politicians know what they can get for their money and hence are better able to prioritise. But this is different in partnerships since there are no given political policies to be implemented. Partnerships cannot be simply observed by the political system as an instrument for governance. Rather, they are a political form of constitution. With partnerships, the political system chooses a particular way of *shaping* policy. Partnerships mean deciding on a political form of decision. From a political perspective, the partners in a partnership are not just suppliers of a politically defined service; they share responsibility for the creation of new visions, ideas and purposes within the framework of the partnership. From the perspective of the political system, the partners in a partnership are part of the political, regardless of the legal status of the partners as private legal subjects. Thus, in political terms, partnerships create a form of particular 'policy communities' (Jordan, 1990).

Doing politics through the creation of partnerships represents a fundamental displacement of the self-programming of the welfare state from concerning the reallocation of resources between different welfare areas such as policy for older people, school policy and social policy to concerning the very way in which political problems, solutions and possibilities for development are created. In political terms, when a partnership is established between a municipality, private companies and a voluntary organisation about an inclusive labour market, it is not a question of allocation of resources for predetermined purposes. Rather, it is a question of establishing a space for the articulation of certain kinds of problems in a simultaneous production of the subjects who are to face the problems (or challenges, which is typically the form problems take on in partnerships). Partnerships result in a particular form of explosion of the political communication into the private sector where voluntary organisations and private companies are made subjects of common partnership concerns. It is a question of private policy (Andersen et al, 1992, pp 122-6).

Thus, partnerships lead to a multiplication of the political and therefore also concern the possibility of the political system to produce and observe itself as a unity. And precisely in the context of partnerships we see the outline of a new semantics of self-description for the political. Above all, it creates concepts for the political that do not limit the political system to a particular societal sector. The concepts of 'municipality', 'state' and 'region' are all sector-defining self-descriptions that indicate a boundary between politics and society. But the emergent tendency, in the context of partnerships, to distance themselves from self-descriptions such as 'welfare state' and a preference for concepts such as 'welfare society' dissolves the boundary between politics and society as a territorial distinction that instead comes to indicate a territorially imploded but logically delimited form of responsibility. Likewise, we see a new tendency to employ the concept of 'network state' not only as a scientific-analytical concept, but as a concept used by many municipalities in their self-descriptions when reflecting on themselves in contexts where many of their activities and much policy development happens through partnerships with voluntary organisations, associations and private companies.

Partnerships as segmented markets

The construction in the *economic system of communication* of partnerships is also different from the construction of first-order contracts. From an economic perspective, a first-order contract is an exchange. A partnership, on the other hand, is observable as an exchange of future possibilities of exchange from an economic point of view. In economic terms, partnerships are about the development of future possible transactions. They represent a transactional transaction. To the extent that a transaction can be said to take place between a buyer and a seller, a partnership as an exchange of possible exchanges can be said to represent an exchange of buyer–seller relations, that is, a second-order exchange is an exchange of exchange relations. What is exchanged is a mutual allocation of energy towards future exchanges.

Since the beginning of the 1980s when the concept of partnership was primarily employed as a term for long-term relations between private companies, we have seen the development of a comprehensive semantic reservoir for economic observations of this kind of exchange of possibilities for exchange with terms such as, for example, 'user–producer relations', 'company network', 'organised market', 'vertical and horizontal value chains', and so on. A common distinction in this semantics is between the exchange of services and products on the one hand, and the exchange of information on the other. Any exchange of products and services also includes an implicit exchange of information. However, in a description of the economic relation as a network relation or partnership, the information side is marked as the central exchange, which increases the possibility for mutual exchange and innovation (see, for example, Williamson, 1975, 1985; Håkansson, 1987; Lundvall, 1988).

Partnerships as programmes for development

Moreover, in relation to the *interpretation by the performance systems* of partnerships, we see a double figure. In the context of public outsourcing it is important that the contract can be read as a performance programme. In relation to partnerships, the central concern is that partnerships function as a programme for the creation of programmes. They represent second-order programmes, particularly in the form of development programmes for new future performance.

Partnerships rarely spell out specific objectives. Rather, they contain indexical indications of 'values', 'considerations', 'overall objectives' and 'visions', almost devoid of content in order to precisely be able to compel the performance systems to ascribe meaning to the indexes through self-programming. Hence, whether the visions have been met or the objectives achieved becomes less important than whether they have been transformed, circulated and multiplied. In a partnership, it is often not a given which performance system is to be linked up. Partnerships are often open to functionally equivalent responses to the indexes. In that sense partnerships represent open invitations, seeking to establish conditions for the initiation of different communications. Thus, when the aforementioned partnership in Bangladesh indicates that its objective is to increase its population's possibilities for earning an income and finding employment in combination with an effort to fight illiteracy and to create awareness about repression, particularly of women, and other components concerning the environment, nutrition and health, there is obviously not a given solution. It is not even given whether the problems should be articulated as economic, legal, educational, family-related or medical. The objectives function as the background for an open communicative scanning of a *possible* programming of the problems in different function systems.

Partnerships as reflexive law

The legal system also reads first- and second-order contracts differently. From a legal point of observation, a contract is a programme for the assessment of right and wrong. Within the framework of first-order contracts, it is legally possible to distinguish between two forms of contract that correspond to two types of programmes for the assessment of right and wrong: formal and material (or substantial) contracts. This distinction is rather common in contract law and draws parallels to Max Weber's distinction between formal and substantial law.

Gunther Teubner and Helmut Willke further define the difference between formal and material contracts as a difference between programmes aimed at regulating behaviour by means of if/then rules, and programmes aimed at the regulation of social processes by means of means/end rules (Teubner, 1983, 1986; Willke, 1986). A contract is defined as formal if it is constructed around if/then stipulations, for example, if the car is delivered in such and such a condition, at such and such a time, then a certain amount is to be paid to this account before a certain time. The more precise and unambiguous the if/then stipulations, the better prepared the contract is in the case of subsequent conflict development. The more detailed the contract, the easier it is to subsequently decide whether the behaviour of the contract partners is in agreement with the contract stipulations, that is, who is right and wrong according to the contract.

A contract, on the other hand, is defined as material if it is constructed around means/end distinctions in which the end is clearly defined and the means more or less open. Thus, a material contract does not primarily specify the expected behaviour, but instead the objectives according to which the contract partner is expected to work. A material contract is so-called object-oriented and contains a detailed specification of objectives and of how to observe whether the objective has been achieved, for example, the objective being a specific number of train departures a day on specific routes with a specific number of passengers. A material contract grants the supplier a certain freedom of method with respect to the achievement of the objectives. Therefore, the contracts do not need the same level of detail. On the other hand, however, it does not take into consideration the same amount of conflict forms; it only considers conflicts in relation to goals and outputs. In the context of outsourcing or long-term first-order contracts with only relatively complex tasks, the typical contract will consists of a mix of formal and material stipulations.

Things become slightly more complex when we look at second-order contracts. Here, we have to make a distinction between two legal *points of observation* for the reading of contracts, where one point of observation is the external formation of law, for example, in the form of courts, and the other point of observation is the partnership as an independent legal system in which the partners themselves discuss right and wrong in relation to the activities of the partnership.

From the point of observation of 'the external formation of law' there is no distinction between first- and second-order contracts, and contracts are read, therefore, as first-order contracts, which, in addition to if/then rules, consist of *procedural rules*, for example, for third party hearing, shared decision making, organs of cooperation, force majeure, involvement and conflict mediation and settlement. Thus, we can speak of the proceduralisation of contracts (Wiethölter, 1986). Such proceduralisations are prevalent in a number of areas other than partnerships as used in the present book, not least within the building and construction sector where procedures for mediation are often employed (Boserup and Humle, 2001).

In legal terms, when the contract is read as a promise about a promise, the contract becomes self-referential. The law is defined in the first order as an external point of reference for the formation of contracts. What a contract is, what it takes for it to be valid, and so on lies outside the contract itself. The contract is inscribed in an always already established legal order. This pertains to so-called formal contracts as well as material contracts although the law is able to more readily obtain professional, non-legal considerations in cases about the decision of right and wrong in material contracts in assessing whether the objective has been achieved or not. In second-order contracts, it is up to the contract to define itself as a contract, including the contract's external points of reference. As a promise about a promise, a partnership represents an agreement to make new promises as well as an agreement about how to qualify such promises as promises. It is a question not simply of procedures for participation and decision making but more fundamentally about establishing the non-legal discursive consideration that are to be considered in the creation of promises.

When NGO partnerships indicate poverty and equality in development efforts, or when a partnership employs social clauses and refers to the supply portal at the Department of Trade and Industry, it is not a question of assigning to the Department or a particular group of impoverished people specific rights in relation to the contract. Rather, it is a question of establishing reflexive obligations in relation to the creation of promises. The only granting in this context of specific rights would be to different discourses or conceptions that further enable the partners to speak or raise objections on behalf of the discourses (in a different context, Teubner refers to discursive rights; see Teubner, 2000, 2005). When the partnership at Hørsholm Hospital refers to the nutritional guidelines of Frederiksborg municipality, it establishes the formal expectation that the partnership and its partners link up with the discussions of nutrition in the municipality, where its discussion is defined as an acceptable place from which you can criticise and question the conception of objectives in the partnership. The partners can discuss, within the partnership, whether the conception of objectives is right or wrong in relation to the nutritional policies.

Second-order contracts can be read, therefore, as *reflexive programmes* (Teubner, 1983, 1988), which, rather than prescribing specific conduct and objectives of social processes and procedures for influence, prescribe the processes of reflection through which the partnership is developed and translated into new promises and cooperation and through which the partners create themselves as partners for the partnership.

As reflexive obligations, partnerships facilitate the creation of partners by allowing for conflict formation with respect to the considerations and conceptions that are to characterise the partnership. However, such reservations only make sense to the extent that the partners wish to continue the partnership (refer to the point made in Chapter Six (at pp 109-110) about partnership only existing in the process of its creation.

Thus, a partnership establishes its own legal order that is only relevant to the extent that the partnership continues. The partnership states its own legal basis through reference to documents and communication, which is perceived as the partnership's legal source. Perceived as reflexive contractual provisions, the partnership simply facilitates its own capacity for legally codified assessment of its own processes.

The legal perception of first- and second-order contracts respectively can be summarised as follows (see Table 7.3).

Table 7.3: The legal reading of first- and second-order contracts

	First-order contract		Second-order contract
Form	Formal contract	Material contract	Reflexive partnership
Programme	Conditional orientation	Purpose orientation	Procedural orientation (perceived from the first order)/reflexive orientation (perceived from the second order)
Regulatory object	Prescribes behaviour directly whereas the result of the behaviour lies outside the regulation	Prescribes direct results of social processes, but only indirect behaviour and procedures	Prescribes procedures that indirectly prescribe and facilitate, on the second order, self-creation and self-regulation. The result, in turn, is outside the regulation or open
Reservations against conflict	Conflicting behaviour	Conflicting objectives and results	Conflicting considerations and discourses

Conclusion

Contrary to the ideals contained in the semantics of partnerships, partnerships can hardly be said to establish communities across boundaries; they undoubtedly, however, enable structural couplings between different function systems and with qualities that are significantly different from first-order contracts.

The law communicates about first-order contracts as a promise and about second-order contracts as a promise about a promise. The economy communicates about first-order contracts as an exchange and about second-order contracts as an exchange of possibilities for exchange. Politics communicates about first-order contracts as a tool for implementation and about second-order contracts as a political constitutional form. The service-producing systems communicate about first-order contracts as a programme for services and about second-order contracts as a programme for subsequent service programming. This shift from the first to the second order fundamentally changes the character of the structural coupling.

The way in which the partnership establishes couplings results in a logic of multiplication. A partnership cannot only be read politically. Because partnerships can be seen politically as a constitutional form, they create politics. Partnerships multiply the political. A partnership cannot only be read in terms of economics. Precisely because it can be seen as the purchase of subsequent possibilities for exchange, it multiplies the economic communication through the creation of a form of internal partnership economies. And the same applies to the law – precisely because it concerns a promise about a promise, a partnership leads to a multiplication of the legal through the constitution of self-creating legal orders.

In the case of first-order contracts, we maintain at least the fiction of a fixed contract, which we can hold in our hand. First-order contracts represent, in a certain sense, an original text that can be read, albeit differently, by the related function systems. In partnerships, this 'original' plays only an insignificant role. Partnerships represent a coupling without a clear point of fixation. The partnership is fluid. It is a second-order coupling that continually seeks out possibilities for coupling. It is not a given which projects are to be initiated in the partnership. And it is also not a given which considerations and hence which function systems will be coupled by various partnership projects. If a new project is under way in the SUPOTH partnership in Bangladesh, should this project be conceived from an environmental, social empowerment or legal perspective about equality? Partnerships enable a constant scanning of possibilities for initiation for different function systems.

Different function systems have different initiators. The care system is only able to initiate itself if it sees the possibility of making a *diagnosis*. If some of the problems in connection with poverty in Bangladesh can be referred back to a diagnostic question, for example, orphans, then this might initiate the care communication. The educational system cannot initiate itself until something can be seen as a *precondition* for the specific position of a certain actor, for example, if women's poverty can be related to their schooling. Political communication cannot define a theme as political until it can be observed as a *common concern*. If a woman's poverty is simply an individual or particular problem, it cannot be said to be political. It has to somehow be able to be seen as a common concern in order to initiate political communication (Andersen and Born, 2003, 2007). The different initiators of a number of function systems are summarised in Table 7.4 below.

Table 7.4: The different initiators of the function systems

System	Medium	Code	Initiator
Legal system	Current law	Right/wrong	Rights
Educational system	Child	Better/worse education	Preconditions
Political system	Power	Govern/governed	Common concerns
System of love	Anticipation	Loved/not loved	Highly personal declarations
Economic system	Money	Paying/not paying	Products
Care system	Care	To help/not help	Diagnoses

The point is that, in partnerships, you can constantly scan and seek out the possibilities for the initiation of different function systems in relation to partnership projects. In this process, the projects remain alive as opposed to documents that have been written once and for all. The projects assume the form and colour of the function systems that are initiated and of the function systems' media that are inscribed into the projects. Theoretically, therefore, openings are constantly created for initiations of new function systems in relation to the project.

If we look at the partnership at Hørsholm Hospital, for example, and its commitment in relation to hospital food, the partnership contract specified a very broad commitment towards the menu development. The agreement prescribed 'a reasonable possibility for choosing between different menus and different kinds of food'. It also prescribed that the choice of food would depend on developments in 'new patient groups, composition of population and other gradual changes in food requirements'. Moreover, the agreement tied the choice of menu to 'current recommendations for Danish institutional food and the nutritional policies of Frederiksborg municipality', and finally it also required that 'a certain share of products used in the production of food must be organic' (Hørsholm Hospital, 2001b, p 9, part 3). This creates ample opportunity for seeking out the communicative contribution of different function systems to the development of menu choices. Taking a medical perspective on the choice of menus sheds light on the relationship between patient and food and hence on a possible differentiation of the patients according to their diagnoses, and the choice of menu is linked to these diagnoses in various diets. Taking a religious perspective on the choice of menu creates sensitivity to the relationship between faith and food with a possibility for differentiation between different religious beliefs in relation to different choices of menu, produce, preparation and serving. Taking a political perspective of the choice of menu creates sensitivity to the life-political in the dietary habits of the people and a differentiation into organic, vegetarian, traditional, acid-base balanced food, and so on.

However, the thematisation in the different function systems of the choice of menu may also initiate other function systems. The aesthetic function system may observe the fact that the medical function system communicates about the lack of appetite in particular patients that may cause the aesthetic function system to suggest choices of menu on the basis of different types of cooking such as Italian, French or fusion cuisine as a way of appealing to the patient's appetite. And the legal system may perceive of experiments with pork-free menus as a reason to define new rights with respect to choices of menu that do not offend people of faith.

This means that the partnership may obtain what Teubner refers to in a different context as an ultra-cyclical character (Teubner, 1991). The coupling becomes self-feeding because the communication of the different systems in relation to the partnership irritates each other productively into additional communication. A partnership does not represent a dead text that can gradually become fixed through interpretation. Rather, a partnership represents a hyper-text with many different readers who add to the text in reading it so that the text either keeps growing, or peters out and disappears.

Partnerships produce possible couplings between function systems but also create permanent unrest. This has already been touched on in the previous chapter and the way in which partnerships establish their own case, time and sociality pointed out. Partnerships presuppose rather than create frozen structures. The way in which case, time and sociality are created in partnerships depends on the function systems that initiate themselves. For example, on the social dimension, the different function systems clearly offer up different fictions for the involved players so that you can in different ways make yourself a partner for the partnership: partner for care, for education and so on (Andersen and Born, 2005).

However, the way in which partnerships establish couplings is not without cost for the function systems since it seems that the way that the partnerships establish couplings between the function systems implicates the logical boundaries of the individual system. In the political system in which the partnership lets itself be seen as a political constitutional form, the boundary between politics and implementation is put at stake. It simply becomes difficult to distinguish implementation from politics, which has consequences for the placement of responsibility but also for the observation of the political performance. This is what happened, for example, in the example from the NGO partnership in Bangladesh where the overall objectives were overshadowed by the process. In the economic system, the relationship between exchange and scarcity is put at stake. You do not choose partnership because it makes good business sense in the here and now. You join a partnership because of its possibilities for future exchanges. A partnership means to engage in the exchange of exchange relations, and what you receive are possibilities for self-development in relation to others and in relation to the perspectives drawn up by the partnership. Thus, the most important economic motivation for partnerships becomes a form of self-scarcity, homo economicus's self-inflicted scarcity. Partnerships that contain the potential for self-development are interesting. Partnerships that merely indicate a more flexible way of operating are uninteresting. In an economic sense, the act of offering up a partnership to someone means to offer up something or someone to develop oneself up against. Finally, in the legal system it seems to be the relation between the pronouncement of judgement and legal order that is put at stake because the partnership reverses the relation so that partnership comes before legal order. In partnerships, the law is not outside but inside and created by the partnership. Thus, any legal discussion in the partnership becomes a discussion of the continuation and existence of the partnership.

In conclusion, the partnership form seems to hold a potential for creating particular intensity fields of couplings that breed couplings, and thus the emergence of 'cross-sectoral' partnerships represents a significant displacement of the functional differentiation. Partnerships create close couplings as well as decouplings. Partnerships increase the couplings between function systems, but precisely because partnerships in their legal structure provide very limited detail about formal if/then rules and material means/end rules but indicate instead requirements for the reflection of independent programme and goal formation, partnerships also increase the mutual indifference of the function systems. This reinforces the possibility for differentiation and autopoiesis in the function systems at the same time as it means that they *can* be coupled more intensely.

EIGHT

Partnerships as second-order organisations

Up to this point partnerships have been studied in two different ways: as second-order contracts and as structural coupling. Subsequently we have explored what this means for the character of the partnership as structural coupling between different function systems, and concluded that there are significant differences in the potential of first- and second-order contracts to establish structural couplings. In this chapter we explore the relation between contract and organisation in relation to partnerships, putting important constitutive conditions at stake. As it is, second-order contracts seem to be able to simultaneously function as a contract and as an organisation. Partnerships seem to represent the impossible figure of self-organising contracts.

The literature on both contracts and organisations often maintains a distinction between them. An organisation represents a *system* for decision making. A contract represents a *relation* of exchange.

In a systems-theoretical sense, an organisation can be seen as a system of communication that communicates through the operation of decision, creates itself through its decisions and consists solely of a network of decided premises for decision. Organisations are nothing more than an accompanying by-product of the unfolding of decision as form. Organisations and their elements are established through decision communication when decisions confirm decisions and turn them into premises for decision. 'What' an organisation is and consists of becomes a result of the way in which organisations deparadoxify decisions and translate them into premises for decision. The point is that organisation systems create themselves through decisions and what a decision is is also established through decisions. Therefore, a decision as the system's formative operation also creates itself. This is the autopoiesis of organisations. No element in an organisation is the product of anything but the unfolding of the decision paradox. A decision decided itself by deciding on premises for decision, and the decision of these premises causes the organisational system to emerge as the unity of decision connections. It remains an open question how a premise becomes a premise. This varies from one organisation to the next, but the historical conditions of possibility for the construction by organisations of premises are also changed through changes in the language, the semantics, which the decision communication has at its disposal. However, four typical premises are highlighted here: an organisational system establishes its *boundary* for the validity of decisions through the definition of membership, including what membership means and who qualifies as member. An organisational system establishes its own *purpose* through the decision of some kind of programme for what it is going to make decisions about, even if it is not particularly specific or clear what constitutes the factual premise for decision. The third element is differentiation and the coordination of *actions*, for example, in the form of responsibilities, positions and staff, which make up the social premise for decision. And finally, the *form of decision* represents a premise for decision that has to be decided in order for the organisation to establish its boundary, its programme and its staff (Luhmann, 1993a, 2000b; Andersen, 2003d). The autopoiesis of the organisational system is illustrated below in Figure 8.1 with decision as the autopoietic operation.

Figure 8.1: Organisation as an autopoietic system

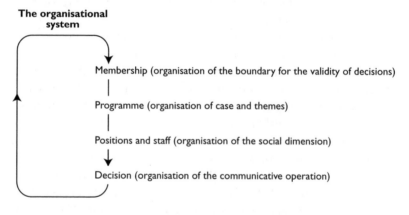

The organisational system

Membership (organisation of the boundary for the validity of decisions)

Programme (organisation of case and themes)

Positions and staff (organisation of the social dimension)

Decision (organisation of the communicative operation)

But are organisations entirely closed? They are in the sense that all their elements are premises for decision, which in order to be premises for decision have to have been decided. However, this closure also opens up the organisation, although never in a way so that something 'foreign' may pervade it. Organisations are open in the sense that they are able to communicate about the external environment and thereby observe the external environment. But they always observe the world from the perspective of an established horizon that decided what they could see and could not see, and they are never able to see what they cannot see. Or put differently, decision communication can obtain information about the environment, but this information is nothing in itself. It is not an essence. In the words of Bateson, information is a difference that makes a difference for a subsequent event in the system (Bateson, 1984). That is, information is always systems relative. Information is not able to simply cross the organisational boundary (Luhmann, 2000a, pp 15–22). It does not represent external input but has to be produced by the organisational system itself as information. In the context of decision communication, information always represents a difference that makes a difference in relation to subsequent decision communication, that is, it appears as a specific type of premise for decision – and premises are, as we mentioned, always already decided premises.

Thus, if we choose to adopt a systems-theoretical perspective, an organisation can be seen as a specific autopoietic system of communication whereas contracts do not possess the self-creating character of the system. However, contracts are also not a relation between organisations as it is assumed in most traditional organisational theory. There are no 'in-between' systems. As we mentioned earlier, a contract represents a structural coupling, and as such it is nothing in itself but only through its simultaneous production as an element in several systems. A contract is an element that is simultaneously produced in at least two systems at once. From the point of observation of the organisation system this means that the relation between organisation and contract always represents an internal relation inside the individual organisation, but that it has to be an internal relation in a system-simultaneous way. The distinction between organisation and contract is a distinction *in* the decision communication of the organisational system where the contract side of the difference is indicated in the organisation when an organisation decides to link up with others and thus to turn the decisions of other organisations into a premise for its own internal decisions. Obviously, a contract does not exist until at least two organisations simultaneously link up with each other through internal decision operations. This can be illustrated in two different ways. First, it can be illustrated by showing the contract as the tangential point where two circles (systems) touch each other at a point without intersecting (see Figure 8.2).

Figure 8.2: The contract as tangential coupling of organisations

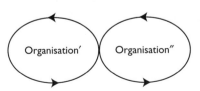

It can also, however, be illustrated in terms of formal logic as two simultaneous operations where the relation between organisation and contract is one (and two) that is simultaneously drawn up in two organisational systems (see Figure 8.3).

Figure 8.3: The relationship between organisation and contract

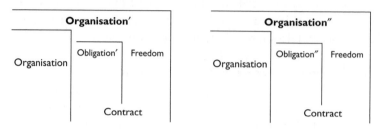

However, partnerships as second-order contracts challenge this figure. As we have already discussed, second-order contracts define the framework for the further development of first-order contracts. Quite a few second-order contracts even define an independent management for the partnership with an accompanying organisation, which is to continually pursue the purpose of the second-order contract about the definition of new contractual relations. Therefore, second-order contracts represent a rather peculiar figure in relation to the distinction between organisation and contract. It seems obvious to ask whether partnerships are actually contracts, which has been maintained up until now, or whether partnerships actually represent a particular system for decision making. Partnerships are peculiar because they represent a form of contractual organisation of contractualisation.

With a first-order contract an organisation decides to promise another organisation to use something in the future as its premise for present decisions. In partnerships, a decision is made about the establishment of premises for the above decisions about connecting to other organisations, placed within the partnership. With the partnership as a second-order contract, an organisation decides to define the future decisions of a partnership with respect to future contractual possibilities as the decision premise in the present in the expectation that the other partners in the partnership will do the same.

In the growing debate on hybrid forms we might find a satisfying answer. Vincent-Jones distinguishes between internal hybrid organisations and external hybrid organisations as different forms of hybrids mixing market and hierarchy (Vincent-Jones, 1997). Gunther Teubner's numerous analyses of hybrids provide a fruitful answer that enables us, moreover, to understand a range of specific empirical demonstrable characteristics of many partnerships. Building on Teubner's argument, it is suggested that we see partnerships as the re-entry of the difference between organisation/contract on the side of contract (Teubner, 1993, 2002). Partnerships represent the re-entry of organisation into the contract. This can also be illustrated in two different ways. This time the figure of formal logic is presented first, which regrettably now becomes so complex that its usefulness becomes dubious (see Figure 8.4).

Figure 8.4: Partnership as re-entry of a distinction

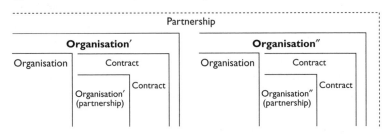

Figure 8.4 seeks to formalise the way in which the difference organisation/contract is re-entered on the contract side so that the organised and systemic elements themselves come to be a part of the relative and coupling elements. In terms of formal logic, this is a paradox because it means that the same appears in what is different. Non-A emerges in A=A. If that were merely a problem of formal logic, it would not matter, but what Teubner asserts is that it installs a logical conflict in the very operating principle of the partnership, a conflict with rather interesting functions (Teubner, 1996, p 60). It means that partnerships are at the same time both organisation and contract. And it means that partnerships are at once an element in the organisational system and their own organisational system.

If we try to illustrate this with the tangential circles, as earlier, a partnership looks Figure 8.5.

Here, one of the aspects of the paradox becomes rather obvious. Figure 8.5 demonstrates that a contractual relation between a number of mutually autonomous organisational systems has itself taken on the character of system. To the extent that partnerships in second-order contracts are assigned an independent management, for example, the partnership is no longer merely a relation between organisations, but is itself an organisation that can create itself and its own purpose.

Figure 8.5: Partnership as a hyper-circle

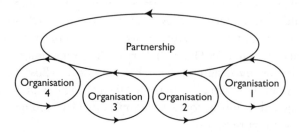

These organisations, however, are of a very specific kind. They become second-order organisations that only exist by virtue of first-order organisations. As a second-order organisation, the partnership becomes a kind of parasite (Teubner, 2002, p 321). A partnership has to live off its host organisation, but it is not dependent on resources from first-order organisations. Partnerships are primarily parasites in the sense that the partnership does not become an organisation until it is produced simultaneously in the internal communication of the first-order organisations as a contract and is given the status of decision premise. The decisions of a partnership depend on a dual retrospective ascription of decision character since it is not until the partners have independently decided to acknowledge the decisions of the partnership as decisions that they become decisions. If the partnership talk is not observed by the first-order organisations as premises for their decisions, it can never be anything but talk (and therefore not decision). Thus, partnerships are condemned to being parasites. They live off the communicational surplus in the member organisations.

This leads us to a very central aspect of partnerships' conditions for functioning as partnerships, an aspect that not only has theoretical value but that is also empirically highly productive. First of all, the above analysis enables us to define empirical criteria for when we talk about partnerships. The criterion is: when first-order organisations give status to their partnerships by observing their communication as their own decision premises. Second, we now have a language that is able to describe what goes wrong in many partnerships.

In her PhD dissertation, Jeanet Hardis followed a number of multipartite partnerships over a period of a few years. A number of them did not live beyond the enthusiastic start-up phase. Two examples of partnerships are referred to next that never actually became partnerships because the partners did not confirm the partnership as an internal decision premise.

On of the cases was the company network in Vestsjælland county (Hardis, 2004, pp 176-225). The partnership was established in May 2000 and consisted of four municipalities, the Confederation of Danish Employers, the Danish Confederation of Trade Unions and 10-12 companies. The goal was to boost the development of the inclusive labour market. The partnership ended only two years later in June 2002. The partnership had been given its own organisation. A central institution in the collaboration was 'the roundtable talks' that were to facilitate dialogue between the main character (the potentially excluded employee), the company and the public help system. Moreover, the partnership had its own steering committee and a network group, and two consultants were hired to develop the partnership and act as project managers. These consultants were placed in the municipalities. The project managers repeatedly tried to propose themes and suggestions for development in the partnership, but the partners only acted on the project managers' communication suggestions to a very limited degree. The companies observed what went on in the partnership but did not commit to it. The expectation was that it would be up to the companies to decide their level of and premises for involvement in the partnership. The project managers introduced a number of initiatives with the purpose of developing the partnership and its strategy, but there was basically no real involvement in the first-order organisations. Therefore, the two consultants left the project after a short period since no one had made a commitment towards their initiatives. The collaboration never became a partnership in the above sense. The partnership contract contained certain second-order aspects, but it was never given a life of its own. The partnership never developed into an independent system and was continually observed as irrelevant noise for the partners.

In another of Hardis's cases, one of the first-order organisations assumed the function of the partnership, which meant that the partnership became a one-sided collaboration. The one organisation basically no longer needed the others in order to establish its decision as decision. The case was a social partnership in Herlev municipality (Hardis, 2004, pp 138-76). The partnership was formally established in September 2000 between the municipality and the company Ruko A/S. The purpose was collaboration with the goal of ensuring that employees did not lose their jobs due to health issues or personal problems – it was about avoiding health-related exclusion from the labour market. The collaboration was implemented in a partnership agreement and became institutionally based in a contact group between the municipality and the company. Thus, the contact group was thought to represent the partnership's independent organisation and was made up of a number of representatives from the company and a social consultant hired by the municipality to be in charge of the partnership function. Part of the function of the contact group was described as ensuring the development of the partnership, structuring the collaboration with the municipality consultant, collection of experience data and dissemination of the partnership and the dialogue about health issues to the entire company. The human resources director in the company saw himself as the actual leading force in the partnership and personally made the decision that the contact group was unnecessary. Ruko saw the contact group as an undesirable organisational element outside the company's existing management and decision-making structure. The municipality consultant was invited to meetings in the company on several occasions but always on the company's initiative. Incidentally, the consultant quickly began to see himself as the company's internal representative in the municipality. The conclusion was that the partnership in fact became an internal management tool at Ruko, sponsored by the public (Hardis, 2004, p 171). No real second-order contract emerged in the partnership.

The point is, therefore, that partnerships, as second-order contracts, re-enter the organisation as an aspect of contract, thus enabling second-order organisation. This simultaneity of second-order contracts and organisations is summarised in Figure 8.6.

Figure 8.6: Contract and second-order organisation

Partnership	
Second-order contracts • A promise about future promises • Presentation of future presentiations of the future with reference to shared future scenarios • Descriptions of factual perspectives on the suspended case	**Second-order organisation** • Strategy (decision about decisions) • Establishment of future scenarios as shared premises • Boundaries in the capacity of shared destiny
First-order contracts • A promise • Presentation of the future • Specification of the specific object of exchange	**First-order organisation** • Decision • Establishment of case • Formal boundaries

It has been shown how second-order contracts define time, case and sociality differently from first-order contracts, for example, the way that first-order contracts are not simply defined as a promise but as a promise about a promise. Similarly, we see a shift in the self-creation of the organisation from the first to the second order. First-order organisations have formal boundaries. Second-order organisations are primarily defined as shared destiny. First-order organisations make decisions about specific cases and problems. Second-order organisations make decisions about reference to future scenarios and visions. First-order organisations create themselves through decision making. Second-order organisations create themselves through strategy development, where strategy means decisions about horizons for planning of future decisions. In this way, strategy becomes an attempt to control the decision making of the first-order organisations. But basically, only first-order organisations are able to decide whether they choose to see the strategy building of second-order organisations as the premise for their own decisions (Andersen, 1995). Thus, partnerships contain a paradox that destabilises them and might reduce them to disconnected second-order talk.

What, then, are the benefits of partnerships? What can be the function of such paradoxical hybrids? Why do they exist? Gunther Teubner argues that partnerships exist because of a special quality that is their ability to carry out opposing expectations. When seen as the re-entering of the difference between organisation/contract on the contract side, there are three functions of partnerships that neither contracts nor organisations are able to carry out on their own.

The first function concerns dual ascription of action (Hutter and Teubner, 1996). A partnership makes it possible for the same action, for example, an initiative preventing someone suffering from long-term illness to be excluded from the labour market by assigning an easier job function to that person, to be ascribed to the partnership as a joined action but also to be ascribed to a number of individual players in the partnership as their specific action. The municipality can refer to their strategy for an inclusive labour market and claim it to be their work. The company can refer to their values and point to their contribution both to a more humane personnel policy and towards carrying a societal responsibility. Thus, a partnership enables different activities to become included in the decision-making processes and self-descriptions of different organisations.

The second function concerns sensitivity with respect to the external environment. Precisely because a partnership involves the possibility of dual ascription of action, it creates an enormous increase in the partners' sensitivity to their environment (Teubner, 1996, p 62). Through a partnership with a voluntary organisation, a municipality obtains access to an entirely different environment, which consists, among other things, of a great number of voluntary and engaged individuals. The voluntary organisation, in turn, obtains access to political lobbyism. Through partnership with a voluntary organisation, a private company, for example, in the area of bio-genetics, obtains access to current critical discussions and may as a result be able to respond before particular media stories appear.

The third function concerns doubletalk. Partnerships can be the answer to opposing demands and expectations. The notion of public–private partnerships (PPPs) is generally considered the successor of outsourcing. The hope is to use PPPs to at once create a greater market and more collective responsibility. The message of outsourcing was: compete. The message to PPPs seems to be both: compete and collaborate (Teubner, 1996, p 61, 2002, p 323). Partnerships enable the coexistence of multiple identities. A partnership gives a private company the possibility of oscillating between seeing itself as an independent company and seeing itself as part of a shared destiny. If we look at the partnerships between public and voluntary organisations, we can observe a similar structure. Here, the double-binding message seems to be: obey as well as be independent. Voluntary organisations in partnerships are at once implored to assume their place in the welfare state. At the same time, it is said that their place in the welfare state is also to be critical towards and independent of the public sector (see also la Cour, 2003, 2005). Again we see how this enables the voluntary organisation to oscillate between two mutually exclusive self-descriptions: voluntary organisations are able to see themselves as taking on social responsibility and transforming the welfare state in the direction of a welfare society by being part of partnerships. But voluntary organisations can also see themselves as fundamentally non-public and non-market, that is, independent, something unique, that no one else is.

Conclusion

How are partnerships articulated? How specifically do partnerships operate communicatively? How are certain spaces of possibility opened up and put at stake in partnerships?

- How are partnerships articulated as interorganisational relations that cut across sectoral boundaries? This question was about the possibilities for communication that the concept of partnership opens up inside the individual organisational system for discussing and developing expectations of internal organisational issues. The analysis showed how a multiplicity of expectations became condensed into the concept of partnership. These included expectations about the partnership as an alternative to outsourcing, an alternative to sectoral break-ups, an alternative to state, market and civil society respectively, and also a mediator between these. Moreover, expectations were articulated about partnerships as the answer to the current problems of the welfare state and its transformation into a welfare society. Furthermore, partnerships were seen as an adequate way of creating commitment in a complex and changeable society and as a way to open up public markets. In this enormous condensation of expectations into the partnership concept, a contract was defined as the counterconcept that kept the many expectations in place. A contract was everything that partnership was not supposed to be: short term, raw outsourcing, different intentions among contract partners, control-based, conflict-ridden, and so on.
- Then the ISS Catering case was used to show how modern outsourcing of public services to private companies led to communicative clashes between different function systems, particularly clashes between economic communication and political communication, amplified by various mass media games. It was shown how outsourcing creates the potential for conflict without establishing a preparedness or a framework for handling the conflicts. In the case of ISS Catering, it was about the fact that the municipality observed ISS through the political code of govern/governed and therefore perceived ISS as a subjacent administrative unit. ISS in turn perceived the relationship with the municipality through the economic code of have/not have and saw the kitchens as their own with full managerial authority. In the clash between the two differently coded communications, there was no unity of disagreement. The municipality and ISS perceived the clashes in radically different ways. This meant that the conflict

became self-contained. It turned into an independent system of conflict that continued to recruit new conflictual themes and slowly consumed more and more attention from the involved parties. The tendency in outsourcing to produce conflicts combined with the lack of framework for handling conflicts basically limits the functionality of outsourcing.

- The way in which the contractual-legal discussion had in fact attempted to develop a contract language in relation to the relational contract was then shown – it counterbalances increasing societal complexity and opens up for communication as an aspect of contracts. It allows for a reading of the contract that is dependent of different professional perspectives in the companies. And it finally opens up for bringing reflexive elements into the contracts in order to ensure a greater level of responsivity. However, these openings all appear within the notion of the law as the neutral grounds on which contracts are developed, grounds that also predefine the contractual partners as subject to the law. The conclusion was that in order to develop a language for partnerships that corresponds with the complexity in which partnerships work, we have to base it, first of all, on a more radical concept of communication and, second, to raise the point of observation up above the law and the other individual systemic perspectives on contracts.

- Subsequently a proposal was developed for a communication and systems theory about contracts. It was argued that contracts could be seen as a specific form of communication that constitutes the unity of obligation and freedom. It was further argued that this form has to necessarily be one of multiplicity so that the construction of the obligation side always depends on the communication systems that gave the obligation a communicative afterlife in the form of commitment. In that light, the unity of contract can be seen as fractionated in an endless game of communication systems, a fractionation that at the same time equips the contract with certain basic qualities as structural coupling between systems.

- On this basis, partnerships were looked at as a specific form and folding of contract. It was shown that, observed as a contractual form, partnerships have to be understood as second-order contracts. Partnerships have to be perceived, therefore, as a functionally equivalent response to a breakdown in the preconditions of first-order contracts. Partnerships stabilise expectations in the expectation of changing expectations. Partnerships describe factual perspectives on a not yet determined subject. Partnerships create their own relevant partners, and, unlike first-order contracts, partnerships create their own preconditions, including their own time, factuality and sociality. Partnerships refer to conditions that are created by them and that are never considered to be stable because a partnership only exists in its current transformation. They simply presuppose that their preconditions are constantly changing. This makes partnerships a second-order social order condemned to always being emerging, to only be in its creation.

- This particular formal quality of partnerships shows itself in the way in which partnerships can function as structural coupling between the function systems of society. Partnerships as second-order contracts are construed by the law as a promise about a promise, by the economy as an exchange of possible exchanges, by the political system as a political constitutional form and by the service-producing systems as a development programme for a future service programme. This gives partnerships an ultra-cyclic character where the coupling becomes self-perpetuating as the different systems' readings of the contract irritate each other productively into further couplings. As coupling, partnerships contain a logic of multiplication. Through partnerships the political in private policy collaborations is multiplied, the economy is multiplied in many internal markets and the law is multiplied in many independent and emerging legal orders. Finally, another unique quality about partnerships seems to be their potential for producing new couplings. The partnership form holds the potential for the creation of particular fields of intensity of couplings between the function systems of society. Partnerships are a coupling-creating coupling, which increases, but does not ensure, the possibilities for productive irritation between function systems.

- Finally it was shown how partnerships as second-order contracts fold the difference between contract and organisation in a way so that the contract obtains self-organising elements. From this point of observation, partnerships can be seen as parasitic second-order organisations that only exist by virtue of first-order organisations. As a second-order organisation, a partnership's decisions come to depend on dual ascription. Not until the partners have independently decided to acknowledge the decisions of the partnership as decisions do they become decisions. That gives partnerships three unique albeit rather fragile functions: (1) a partnership is able to ascribe actions doubly, to the partnership and to the individual partners; (2) partnerships can increase partners' sensitivity to their environment by giving partners access to each other's environments; (3) partnerships enable doubletalk and multiple identities by functioning as the answer to opposing demands and expectations. The message to public–private partnerships (PPPs) seems to be: compete as well as collaborate. In voluntary–public partnerships it is: obey and be independent. The partners are able to oscillate between following one or the other demand. This is the double-binding organisation of second-order organisation.

Thus, a partnership is not merely a new tool in new public management. It is a form of communication that adds new life to contracts as a form, a form that is as old as the form of functional differentiation. Therefore, a partnership is not an island in the social that can be observed in isolation. A partnership points in the direction of greater social changes. Partnerships emerge as a response to the fact that the preconditions of classical contracts are breaking up. A partnership seems to be the answer to: (1) the fact that the mutual dependence of function systems has been increased at the same time as their differentiation has deepened; (2) the fact that there has been an increase in organisations' need for long-term commitment to each other at the same time as growing demands for flexibility and adaptability make it difficult to commit long term; and (3) the fact that the need for interorganisational intensive relations has grown at the same time as sociality has become fluid. Put together, the phenomenon of partnership points to significant dislocations in the practices of the functionally differentiated society.

The reason that partnerships seem to provide a viable answer could be that they hold a certain level of resistance to paradoxes. One might even argue that partnerships distinguish themselves in their ability to assist organisations in managing paradoxes. Teubner says about similar hybrids: 'Under certain conditions, hybrid arrangements can provide for an institutional environment where paradoxical communication is not repressed, not only tolerated, but invited, institutionally facilitated and turned productive' (Teubner, 1996, p 59). This seems to be very much the case in partnerships.

In summary, partnerships can be said to be a peculiarly fragile and restless possibility-creating machine. Normal contracts can be said to consist of voluntary commitment of your freedom. When organisations enter into contracts with other organisations, uncertainty is absorbed with respect to mutual expectations, and the individual organisation is able to perceive the contract as a stable premise for further decision making. For example, now that we have entered this contractual agreement, we are able to make this particular investment. Contracts put restraints on the organisation but also stabilise certain decision premises. A regular contract can be seen as a machine for realisation. It is through contracts that individuals or organisations are able to realise their freedom rights by entering into a relationship of commitment with others. Partnerships are different. A partnership is not a machine for the realisation of possibilities but a machine for the production of possibilities. Partnerships do not represent measurable commitments and do not constitute stable decision premises for the organisations. Rather, it is the reverse. A partnership holds in its form the potential to constantly produce new possibilities for partners and their mutual relations. Partnerships can produce new partners, new visions for the future and ideas for development, and new themes for collaboration and consideration. Partnerships are able to draw the function systems into ultra-cyclic productive disruptions of each other and hence produce a great amount of new possibilities for the involved systems, for the political system in the form of new possibilities for governing, for the economic system in the form of new business opportunities, or for the care system in the form of new possibilities for providing help. As second-order organisations, partnerships can be the producer of interorganisational strategies and thereby provide new occasions for decision making and possibilities for development for the partners. Thus, rather than absorbing uncertainty, partnerships produce contingency. If there is an element of stabilisation and uncertainty-absorption to partnerships, it is on a different level. It ensures a framework for productive disagreement and clashes between heterogeneous communications and expectations. Partnerships make it possible to test out conflicts and search for positive possibilities.

Partnerships are also fragile, however. Nothing ensures their continued existence. They are, as mentioned earlier, an emergent social order. Partnerships can never simply be, but exist only in their creation. Partnerships are always about partner creation, and nothing is as fragile as creation. If the partners do not see the possibilities of partnerships, they cease to exist. Partnerships are fragile possibility-making machines intended for long-term perspectives for the future but deeply dependent on present support and intensity.

To conclude, what might the above teach us in relation to the creation and management of partnerships? What happens if we move the second-order observations down to the first order? If you buy into the partnership language that has been developed here, does that make you able to see something that we might not have paid much attention to before? What are the questions we should pay attention to when engaging in partnerships? It is difficult to provide generally useful answers to these questions, however. First, there are three general 'suggestions', followed by a few dilemmas and challenges for specific organisational types in partnerships. As this might jeopardise the complex insights developed in the book, the following should not be read as comprehensive answers but merely an attempt to lay out a few possible paths and themes.

Three quick general suggestions

Generally speaking, it is important to know how much is at stake when we experiment with partnerships. There is an obvious tendency to use 'just like that' thinking when suggesting partnerships, and therefore there is often much disappointment when the result is not always as desired. Perceived as social innovation, a partnership is not Stone Age technology. It is socially high technology, and, as we generally know, high technology is associated with large investments and development costs. Moreover, it is a form that requires many management resources and significant political-communicative competencies.

Second, partnerships produce new couplings between function systems. Decisions about and operation of partnerships should not fail to take this into account. If partnerships are merely perceived as slightly more flexible and trust-based contracts, you have not made yourself cognitively sensitive to the functionality of partnerships. Any professional involvement with partnership ought to seriously consider the functional communication systems and their specific configuration in the partnership. When developing a PPP about labour market activation, which initiations of functional logics are opened up or shut down? In what way is an educational communication invited or rejected within the specific constellation of activation partnership? Thus it is important to consider when developing a partnership the way in which particular function systems are maintained, perhaps at the expense of other function systems. To strategically think about partnerships is to consider the way in which different function systems and consideration can be linked to it.

Finally, partnerships are fragile possibility-making machines. Which possibilities do you want the partnership to make possible? The object of exchange in partnerships is not primarily money and services. It is primarily possibilities, including possibilities for the self-development of the individual partner. The Danish newspaper *Børsen* recently ran a series of articles about partnerships in which private companies expressed their disappointment. The PPPs that had been initiated since the government intensified its focus on them did indeed break even in an economic sense; however, they did not contain enough long-term perspectives for the companies to maintain an interest in investing management resources in them. Partnerships require strategic ambitions and mutual strategic dependency between the partners or they end up as nothing more than behemoth superstructures on top of first-order contracts and lose their functionality.

To political organisations

From a political perspective, partnerships clearly offer certain potentials. However, it is a very strategically demanding task to focus your efforts on partnerships. As it is, partnerships are not only about transferring responsibilities to private companies or voluntary organisations. If this is the extent of your vision and courage, you ought to stay away from partnerships because this is simply not where their strength lies. Partnerships do not merely entail transferring responsibilities. They also entail transferring policy development, and therefore partnership formations are also, politically speaking, about strategic organisation of political processes and conflict development. From a political perspective, the act of initiating a partnership is a question of inviting a multitude of independent and different organisations across various connections to function systems to enter into an independent form of private policy network. Creating partnerships naturally represents a form of government, but it also means giving up government because, in order for the partnership to work optimally as a partnership, it needs room to create itself and its own agendas. Governing through partnerships involves a form of self-ironical politics that has to accept the fact that once the partnership has been formed, the only thing to do is support its self-government (Wilke, 1992a, 1992b, 1997). Governing through partnership presupposes a 'politic of modesty' that cannot claim for its worldview to work as a role model for the other systems in the partnership. If the political system believes that it alone is able to represent the unity of society, its regulations will soon cause the partnership to end. The precondition for government becomes defining a limit for your own government. In other words, the precondition for government through partnerships is to relinquish intervening government in favour of reflexive government.

To companies

Ever since the privatisation programmes of the early 1980s, private companies have looked to the public sector as a potential market. On several occasions, changing governments have suggested outsourcing on a large scale, at first the more peripheral services of the public sector and subsequently its core services. Each time, many companies have envisioned that a previously closed market worth billions would be opened up to them. But each time they have been disappointed. What was thought to be a grand outsourcing wave became nothing but a ripple, often blocked by individual cases that ended up on the front pages of newspapers and gave the political players cold feet in relation to their plans for outsourcing based on the motto 'better re-elected than efficient'. Outsourcing of public services has proved itself to be a highly risky market for many companies, resulting in unforeseen and uncontrollable conflicts. It draws the company into contexts where there is constant uncertainty about who the company is in fact supposed to do business with. It draws the company into contexts where the company believes to have delivered a good tender that the public purchasing agent would appreciate, a tender that would lead to more calls for tenders, whereas in reality it is often a question of hidden spending cuts where the private company becomes the obvious scapegoat, unable to respond. Perhaps a partnership can give new hope. That requires, however, for private companies not to confuse public markets with other markets. 'Joint responsibility', for example, does not mean the same in economic communication as in political communication. Partnership as a yes to joint responsibility is also a political responsibility. If private companies are to seriously come into play on public markets they have to mimic public companies. If private companies want to work on public markets through partnerships, they have to first create themselves as politically and administratively credible partners. And if companies wish to also be a part of the core areas of the welfare state, for example care or counselling of unemployed people, it is not enough for companies to perceive of care or counselling as services that might lead to increased profits. Companies have to look at themselves from the perspective of care and counselling. They have to establish themselves as care organisations, whose primary function is care, and not just as a provider of care services. If politics, care, and so on are merely seen as insular aspects of the companies (as a product) and the general self-description of the company is just economic, it will not work. Companies have to be able to work with multiple self-descriptions. It is not enough to have an economic strategy. Companies also need to have a strategy for themselves as a political-administrative player, as the creator of welfare and a strategy for themselves as, for example, a central care institution. No unity is able to unify these strategies. This is part of the price that has to be paid when entering 'the public market', characterised by many heterogeneous logics. Management competencies have to be economic, political and welfare-technical. Management competency becomes the ability to switch between many communicative codes without assigning privilege to any one of them. A professional company on a public market is one that is able to overcome professional polyphony.

To voluntary organisations

Partnerships with public as well as private companies clearly represent possibilities for development and expansion to many voluntary organisations. Voluntary organisations are able to gain new sovereignty through partnerships. Becoming a partner in a partnership within one of the core areas of the public welfare state does not only mean becoming a supplier to the public, it also means being recognised as a negotiation partner in the definition of the content of the welfare state. You become the negotiator not only of solutions but also of the character of the problems and the horizon for the development of a particular welfare area. And this provides an opportunity for the voluntary organisation to develop itself, its identity and its efforts through partnerships. But partnerships also represent the opportunity for the other partners to influence the self-creation of the voluntary organisation. Voluntary organisations' invitation to partnership with the public is always an invitation in the political medium of power. From the perspective of the political system, the voluntary organisation is always one to be governed. This is the case even when the invitation is in the name of dialogue with an emphasis on empowerment and capacity building. Empowerment represents the doubling of the code of power. Basically, empowerment is a question of governing self-government. Empowerment divides those who are being observed into those who are empowered and the powerless. Empowerment means to empower the powerless in the empowering agent's own image of what it means to be empowered. Hence, when the public observes voluntary organisations from this perspective, it does not amount to the renunciation of control; on the contrary, it is an expression of the fact that the public seeks to help the voluntary organisation to create itself in a particular way. That is what policies of voluntariness are about. The challenge to the voluntary organisation consists in finding out how to operate in such a space so that the organisation is recognised as empowered and yet is still in control of its own self-creation. Thus, partnerships with the public require a very high level of internal strategic and management capacity in the voluntary organisation in order not to be created merely in the image of the partnership but to be created in the image of the partner (la Cour, 2002, 2003, 2005).

To universities

One of the prevalent trends in the university world is closer collaboration with the rest of society in general and the business world in particular. Currently, we see the exploration of many possibilities for cooperation, and one of those is partnerships, a solution backed by many international organisations such as the Organisation for Economic Co-operation and Development (OECD) and the World Bank. A partnership between a university and the business community should be based on the mutual understanding that the partners fundamentally do not understand each other. Things can go fundamentally wrong if the research side expects knowledge to mean the same to the private company as it does to the research institution. Knowledge in the scientific communication system has two sides: function and utility. Function refers to the way in which science itself understands knowledge. To science, knowledge is a goal in itself. Knowledge is its own function, and the scientific system justifies the need for new knowledge with the knowledge of non-knowledge. Scientific communication does not need an external reference in order to justify a research project. This can be traced even to the way in which research articles are constructed in international journals. The articles almost always begin with an overview of previous articles in the field. After that, the articles identify an area of non-knowledge that has not been covered by the mentioned articles, and this 'hole' becomes the justification for the current article. Thus, science is self-referring and self-creating: new studies are justified solely through reference to themselves. To the rest of the communication systems of society, however, this is uninteresting. To the rest of society's systems, knowledge is not a function in itself but a utility in relation to another function. Thus, knowledge as performance refers to the way in which other communication systems perceive of research-produced knowledge. An organisation, for example, is only interested in knowledge if it functions as a decision premise. A political institution is primarily interested in knowledge if it supports its political programme, or, even better, if it is able to cast doubt on the opponent's programme. To a training institution, knowledge is primarily interesting if it can be seen as a qualification that course participants have to acquire, and so on. This distinction between two perceptions of knowledge is challenged in a partnership between a university and a private company. In a close research partnership it is generally expected that the science-produced knowledge can also be seen as useful for the non-scientific partner. Many things can go wrong if none of the partners acknowledge this difference between knowledge as function and knowledge as utility.

And the same applies if only the research institution is able to observe this difference. If the research institution does not remain on the function side and wants to also be responsible for the utility side, it might lead to a structural corruption of the research institution. It will be forced to oscillate between the scientific code and the code of the partner. The result may be that the product may indeed be able to be seen as utility for the private partner but that it has no value in the scientific communication and that the research institution has distorted its attention and resources away from what is scientifically relevant. Partnerships between universities and society may intensify productive irritation of each other. For example, it might be useful for research to be able to observe the way in which its partners perceive its knowledge externally. However, in order for this to happen it is important not to confuse partnership with community.

Partnerships are possibility-creating machines. They can be used as accelerators for partners' development. They are, however, also *fragile* possibility-creating machines. They concern the future and paradoxically, therefore, their future probably is not long. They have to be continually created and recreated, which increases the risk that they become dissolved. This is not a problem, however. Here, too, serial monogamy applies.

References

Andersen, N.Å. (1995) *Selvskabt forvaltning: Forvaltningspolitikkens og centralforvaltningens udvikling i Danmark 1990-1994* (*Autopoietic administration: The history of administrative policy and central administration in Denmark 1990-1994*), Copenhagen: Nyt fra Samfundsvidenskaberne.

Andersen, N.Å. (1996) *Udlicitering - Når det private bliver politisk* (*Contracting out: When the private turns political*), Copenhagen: Nyt fra Samfundsvidenskaberne.

Andersen, N.Å. (1997) *Udlicitering – Strategi og historie* (*Contracting out – strategy and history*), Copenhagen: Nyt fra Samfundsvidenskaberne.

Andersen, N.Å. (2000) 'Public market – political firms', *Acta Sociologica*, vol 43, no I, pp 43-62.

Andersen, N.Å. (2003a) *Borgerens kontraktliggørelse* (*Contractualisation of the citizen*), Copenhagen: Hans Reitzels Forlag.

Andersen, N.Å. (2003b) 'Polyphonic organisations', in T. Hernes and T. Bakken (eds) *Autopoietic organization theory*, Liber & Abstract, Oslo: Copenhagen Business School Press, pp 151-82.

Andersen, N.Å. (2003c) *Discursive analytical strategies – Understanding Foucault, Koselleck, Laclau, Luhmann*, Bristol: The Policy Press.

Andersen, N.Å. (2003d) 'The undecidability of decision', in T. Hernes and T. Bakken (eds) *Autopoietic organization theory*, Liber & Abstract, Oslo: Copenhagen Business School Press, pp 151-82.

Andersen, N.Å. (2004a) 'Supervisionsstaten og den politiske virksomhed' ('The supervision state and the political firm'), in C. Frankel (ed) *Virksomhedens politisering*, Copenhagen: Forlaget Samfundslitteratur.

Andersen, N.Å. (2004b) 'The contractualisation of the citizen – on the transformation of obligation into freedom', *Social Systems*, vol 10, no 2, pp 273-91.

Andersen, N.Å. (2007) 'Creating the client who can create himself and his own fate – the tragedy of the citizens' contract', *Qualitative Sociology Review*, vol III, no 2, pp 119-43, see www.qualitativesociologyreview. org/ENG/Volume7/QSR_3_2_Andersen.pdf

Andersen, N.Å. and Born, A. (2000) 'Complexity and change: two "semantic tricks" in the triumphant oscillating organization', *System Practice and Action Research*, vol 13, no 3, pp 297-328.

Andersen, N.Å. and Born, A. (2003) 'Shifters', in H. Højlund and M. Knudsen (eds) *Organiseret kommunikation – systemteoretisk analyse*, Copenhagen: Samfundslitteratur, pp 182-206.

Andersen, N.Å. and Born, A. (2005) 'Selvet mellem undersøgelse og bekendelse – En inklusions- og eksklusionsmaskine' ('The self between investigation and confession – an inclusion and exclusion machine'), *Grus*, no 74, pp 94-114.

Andersen, N.Å. and Born, A. (2007) 'Heterophony and the postponed organisation – organizing autopoietic systems', *Tamara Journal for Critical Organizational Inquiry*, vol 6, no 6.2, pp 176-86.

Andersen, N.Å., Elberg, J., Kjær, P. and Pedersen, O.K. (1992) *Privat politik (Private politics)*, Copenhagen: Samfundslitteratur.

Anderson-Wallace, M., Blatern, C. and Lejk, A. (2000) 'Advances in cross-boundary practice', in T. Taillieu (ed) *Collaborative strategies and multi-organizational partnership*, Leuven-Apeldoorn: Garant Publisher.

Ariés, P. (1982) *Barndommens historie (The history of childhood)*, Copenhagen: Nyt Nordisk Forlag.

AS/3 (2003a) 'Nye opgaver kræver partnerskaber' ('New tasks demand partnerships'), *Ledige i job*, no 3, p 3.

AS/3 (2003b) 'Partnerskab i arbejdsmarkedspolitikken' ('Partnerships in the labour market policy'), *Internt notat*, Århus 6/5.

Bateson, G. (1984) *Ånd og Natur – en nødvendig enhed (Mind and Nature)*, Copenhagen: Rosinante.

Bevis, H. (1932) 'The pitfalls of partnership agreement', *Harvard Business Review*, vol 10, no 3, pp 366-72.

Boserup, H. and Humle, S. (2001) *Mediationsprocessen (The mediation process)*, Copenhagen: Nyt juridisk Forlag.

Callon, M. (1998) 'An essay on framing and overflowing: economic externalities revisited by sociology', in M. Callon (ed) *The laws of the markets*, Oxford: Blackwell Publishers.

Campbell, D. (2000a) 'Reflexivity and welfarism in the modern law contract', *Oxford Journal of Legal Studies*, vol 20, no 3, pp 477-98.

Campbell, D. (2000b) 'The limits of concept formation in legal science', *Social and Legal Studies*, vol 9, no 3, pp 439-47.

Campbell, D. and Harris, D. (1993) 'Flexibility in long-term contractual relationships: the role of co-operation', *Journal of Law and Society*, vol 20, no 2, pp 166-91.

Campbell, J., Hall, J. and Pedersen, O. (2006) *National identity and the varieties of capitalism: The Danish experience*, Copenhagen: DJØF Publishing.

Center for frivilligt socialt arbejde (Centre for Voluntary Social Work) (2003) *Partnerskaber mellem frivillige organisationer og det offentlige på det sociale område (Partnerships between voluntary organisations and the public in the social field)*, Odense.

Center for frivilligt socialt arbejde (Centre for Voluntary Social Work) (2004) *Frivillig*, vol 12, no 72.

Clam, J. (2000) 'System's sole constituent: the operation', *Acta Sociologica*, 43, no I, pp 63-79.

Collins, H. (1992) 'Distributive justice through contracts', in R.W. Rideout and B.A. Hepple (eds) *Current legal problems*, vol 45, part 2, Oxford: Oxford University Press.

Collins, H. (1993) 'The transformation thesis and aspiration of contractual responsibility', in T. Williamsson (ed) *Perspectives of critical contract law*, Aldershot: Dartmouth.

Collins, H. (1999) *Regulating contracts*, Oxford: Oxford University Press.

Cour, A. la (2002) 'Frivillighedens pris' ('The price of volunteer work'), PhD dissertation, dissertation no 21, Sociologisk Institut, Copenhagen.

Cour, A. la (2003) 'Den forlegne organisation' ('The embarrassed organisation'), *Grus*, no 70, pp 62-79.

Cour, A. la (2005) 'Er de frivillige organisationers teknologiunderskud et problem?' ('Do volunteer organisations have a technology deficit?'), *Dansk sociologi*, no 2, pp 27-46.

Cour, A. la and Højlund, H. (2003) 'Care, standardization and flexibility', in T. Hernes and T. Bakken (eds) *Autopoietic organization theory*, Liber & Abstract, Oslo: Copenhagen Business School Press.

Danida (2000a) *Strategi for dansk støtte til civilsamfundet i udviklingslandene – herunder samarbejder med de danske NGO'er* (*Strategy for Danish assistance to civil society in developing countries – Including collaboration with Danish NGOs. Analysis and strategy*), Copenhagen: Danida.

Danida (2000b) *Danmarks udviklingspolitik, strategi. Partnerskab 2000* (*Danish development policy, strategy. Partnership 2000*), Copenhagen: Danida.

Danida (2004a) *Danidas NGO-samarbejde* (*Danida's NGO-collaborations*), Copenhagen: Danida.

Danida (2004b) *De danske NGO'ers folkelige forankring* (*The popular anchorage of Danish NGOs*), Copenhagen: Danida.

Derrida, J. (1988) *The ear of the other*, Lincoln, NE: University of Nebraska Press.

Derrida, J. (1989) 'Babelstårne' ('The tower of Babel'), in T. Eriksen (ed) *Walter Benjamin oversat*, Århus: Slagmark.

Dore, R. (1983) 'Goodwill and the spirit of market capitalism', *British Journal of Sociology*, vol 34, no 4, pp 459-82.

Doyle, M. (2003) 'Discourse of employability and empowerment: foundation degrees and "third way" discursive repertoires', *Discourse: Studies in the Cultural Politics of Education*, vol 24, no 3, pp 275-88.

Durkheim, É. (1984) *Division of labour in society*, London: Macmillan.

Esposito, E. (1996) 'From self-reference to autology: how to operationalize a circular approach', *Social Science Information*, vol 35, no 2, pp 269-81.

Fenwick, T.J. (2004) 'Discursive work for educational administrators: tensions in negotiating partnerships', *Discourse: Studies in the Cultural Politics of Education*, vol 25, no 2, pp 171-87.

Flyverbom, M. (2006) *Making the global information society governable: On the governmentality of multi-stakeholder networks*, PhD Series, Copenhagen: Copenhagen Business School.

Foucault, M. (1972) 'The discourse on language', in M. Foucault, *The archaeology of knowledge*, New York, NY: Pantheon Books.

Foucault, M. (1993) *Diskursens ordning (The order of discourse)*, Stockholm: Brutus Östlings Bokförlag.

Foucault, M. (1998) 'On the archaeology of sciences: response to the epistemology circle', in M. Foucault, *Aestetics, method, and epistemology*, London: Penguin Books.

Gibson, B., Gregory, J. and Robinson, P.G. (2005) 'The intersection between systems theory and grounded theory: the emergence of grounded systems observer', *Qualitative Sociology Review*, vol 1, no 2, pp 3-20.

Håkansson, H. (ed) (1987) *Industrial technology development: A network approach*, London: Croom Helm.

Hardis, J. (2001) 'Er det "hot" eller "not"? – Om skabelsen af fænomenet "sociale partnerskaber"' ('Is it hot or not? On the making of the phenomenon of social partnerships'), *Grus*, no 65, pp 46-68.

Hardis, J. (2004) *Sociale partnerskaber: Et socialkonstruktivistisk casestudie af partnerskabsaktørers virkelighedsopfattelse mellem identitet og legitimitet*, (*Social partnerships: A case study of partnership actors' worldviews between identity and legitimacy from a social constructivism perspective*) PhD Serie 6, Forskerskolen Viden og Ledelse, Copenhagen: CBS, Samfundslitteratur.

Højlund, H. (2004a) 'Kontraktparadokser i den kommunale organisation' ('The paradoxes of contracts within the organisation of municipalities'), in M. Knudsen and H. Højlund (ed) *Organiseret kommunikation*, Copenhagen: Samfundslitteratur.

Højlund, H. (2004b) *Markedets politiske fornuft: Et studie af velfærdens organisering i perioden 1990-2003* (*The political sense of market: A study of the organisation of welfare 1990-2003*), Copenhagen: Samfundslitteratur.

Højlund, H. and Højlund, C. (2000) 'Velfærdsparadoks og kommunikation: "fælles sprog": en anden ordens strategi på hjemmehjælpsområdet' ('Welfare paradoxes and communication: "Common language": a strategy of second order on the home care area'), *Grus*, no 61, pp 18-39.

Hørsholm Hospital (2001a) *Udbudsbetingelser og vejledning til tilbudsgivere* (*Conditions of tenders and guidelines for bidders*), Hørsholm.

Hørsholm Hospital (2001b) *Udkast til partnerskabskontrakt om varetagelse af serviceopgaver på Hørsholm Sygehus* (*Draft to a partnership contract about service task at Hørsholm Hospital*), Hørsholm.

Hørsholm Hospital (2002) 'Partnerskab mellem Hørsholm Sygehus og ISS' ('Partnerships between Hørsholm Hospital and ISS'), Internal document, Torben Knudsen 27 September.

Hovgaard, T. (2002) 'Supoth – Kapacitetsopbygning af jordløse bønder i Bangladesh' ('Supoth – Capacity development regarding landless farmers in Bangladesh'), Projektrådgivningen, Århus, see www.projektraadgivningen.org/downloads/supoth.pdf

Hutter, M. and Teubner, G. (1996) 'The parasitic role of hybrids', in D. Campbell and P.Vincent-Jones (eds) *Contract and economic organisation*, Aldershot: Dartmouth.

Industriministeriet (1989) *Strategi 92*, Erhvervspolitisk redegørelse, Copenhagen.

ISS (2002) 'Partnerskab på Hørsholm Sygehus' ('Partnership at Hørsholm Hospital') (Torben Knudsen) in the pamphlet: *Nye mål –nye muligheder: Debat om offentligt-privat samarbejde*, ISS, Copenhagen.

Jessop, B. (1999) 'The dynamics of partnership and governance failure', in G. Stoker (ed) *The new politics of local governance in Britain*, Oxford: Oxford University Press.

Jordan, A.G. (1990) 'Sub-governments, policy communities and networks', *Journal of Theoretical Politics*, vol 2, no 3, pp 319-38.

Kjær, P., Andersen, N.Å. and Pedersen, O.K. (2001) *Mandag morgen i det politiske kommunikationssystem* (*'Monday Morning' in the political communication system*), CCC Working Paper No 7, Copenhagen: CBS.

Klemm, J. and Glasze, G. (2005) 'Methodische probleme Foucault-inspirierter diskursanalysen in den sozialwissenschaften', *Forum Qualitative Social Research*, vol 6, no 2, article 24.

Koselleck, R. (1985) *Futures past*, Cambridge, MA: MIT Press.

Kurunmäki, L. and Miller, P. (2004) *Modernisation, partnership and the regulation of risk,* Working Paper No 100504, London: London School of Economics and Political Science.

Ling, T. (2000) 'Unpacking partnership: the case of health care', in T. Taillieu (ed) *Collaborative strategies and multi-organizational partnership,* Leuven–Apeldoorn: Garant Publisher.

Luhmann, N. (1981) 'Communication about law in interactions systems', in K. Knorr-Cetina and A.V. Cicourel (ed) *Advances in social theory and methodology: Toward and integration of micro- and macro-sociologies,* London: Routledge and Kegan Paul.

Luhmann, N. (1988a) 'Frauen, Männer und George Spencer Brown', *Zeitschrift für Soziologie,* vol 17, no 1, pp 47-71.

Luhmann, N. (1988b) *Erkenntnis als konstruktion,* Bern: Benteli Verlag.

Luhmann, N. (1989) *Ecological communication,* Chicago, IL: University of Chicago Press.

Luhmann, N. (1990a) 'The cognitive program of constructivism and a reality that remains unknown', in E. Krohn (ed) *Selforganization: Portrait of a scientific revolution,* Dordrecht: Kluwer Academic Publishers.

Luhmann, N. (1990b) 'The autopoiesis of social systems', in N. Luhmann, *Essays on self-reference,* New York, NY: Columbia University Press.

Luhmann, N. (1990c) *Political theory in the welfare state,* New York, NY: Walter de Gruyter.

Luhmann, N. (1992a) 'Operational closure and structural coupling', *Cardozo Law Review,* vol 13, no 5, pp 1419-41.

Luhmann, N. (1992b) 'The coding of the legal system', in A. Teubner and G. Febbrajo (eds) *State, law, and economy as autopoietic systems,* Milan: Dott. A. Giuffré Editore.

Luhmann, N. (1993a) 'Die paradoxie des entscheidens', *Verwaltungs-Archiv. Zeitschrift für Verwaltungslehre, Verwaltungsrecht und Verwaltungspolitik,* vol 84, no 3, pp 287-99.

Luhmann, N. (1993b) 'Deconstruction as second-order observing', *New Literary History,* no 24, pp 763-82.

Luhmann, N. (1993c) '"Was ist der Fall" und "Was steckt dahinter?" Die Zwei Soziologien und die Gesellschafstheorie', *Zeitschrift für Soziologie,* vol 22, no 4.

Luhmann, N. (1993d) *Risk: A sociological theory,* New York, NY: Walter de Gruyter.

Luhmann, N. (1993e) 'Barnet som medium for opdragelse' ('The child as medium'), in J. Cederstrøm, L. Qvortrup and J. Rasmussen (eds) *Læring, samtale, organisation – Luhmann og skolen,* Copenhagen: Unge pædagoger.

Luhmann, N. (1993f) *Gesellschaftsstruktur und semantik*, vol 1, Frankfurt: Suhrkamp.

Luhmann, N. (1995a) 'Why system theory?', *Cybernetics and Human Knowing*, vol 3, no 2, pp 3–10.

Luhmann, N. (1995b) *Social systems*, Stanford, CA: Stanford University Press.

Luhmann, N. (1996) 'On the scientific context of the concept of communication', *Social Science Information*, vol 35, no 2, pp 257-67.

Luhmann, N. (1997) 'Kunstens medie' ('Art as medium'), in N. Luhmann, *Lagttagelse og paradoks*, Copenhagen: Gyldendal.

Luhmann, N. (1999) 'The paradox of form', in D. Backer (ed) *Problems of form*, Stanford, CA: Stanford University Press.

Luhmann, N. (2000a) *The reality of the mass media*, Cambridge: Polity Press.

Luhmann, N. (2000b) *Organisation und entscheidung*, Wiesbaden: Westdeutscher Verlag.

Luhmann, N. (2004) *Law as a social system*, Oxford: Oxford University Press.

Lundvall, B.Å (1988) 'Innovation of an interactive process: from user-producer interaction to national systems of innovation', in G. Dosi (ed) *Technology and economic theory*, London: Francis Pinter.

Maas, A. and Bakker, D.-J. (2000) 'Managing differences in a multi-paradigmatic partnership', in T. Taillieu (ed) *Collaborative strategies and multi-organizational partnership*, Leuven-Apeldoorn: Garant Publisher.

Macaulay, S. (1963a) 'The use and non-use of contracts in the manufacturing industry', *The Practical Lawyer*, vol 9, no 7, pp 13-40.

Macaulay, S. (1963b) 'Non-contractual relations in business: a preliminary study', *American Sociological Review*, vol 28, no 1, pp 55-67.

Macaulay, S. (1985) 'An empirical view of contract', *Wisconsin Law Review*, pp 465-82.

Macaulay, S. (1986) 'Private government', in L. Lipson and S. Wheeler (ed) *Law and social sciences*, New York, NY: Russell Sage Foundation.

Macaulay, S. (1987) 'Et empirisk syn på kontrakter' ('An empirical view on contracts'), in B.-M. Blegvad and F. Collin (eds) *Virksomheden mellem økonomi og jura – om retsøkonomi og styring*, Copenhagen: Samfundslitteratur.

Macaulay, S. (1991) 'Longterm continuing relations: the American experience regulating dealerships and franchises', in C. Joerges (ed) *Franchising and the law*, Baden-Baden: Nomos Verlagsgesellschaft.

Macaulay, S. (2003) 'The real and the paper deal: empirical pictures of relationships, complexity and the urge for transparent simple rules', in D. Campbell, H. Collins and J. Wrightman (eds) *Implicit dimensions of contract*, Oxford: Hart Publishing.

Macaulay, S. (2004) 'Freedom from contract: solutions in search of a problem', *Wisconsin Law Review*, pp 777-820.

Macneil, I.R. (1974) 'The many futures of contracts', *Southern California Law Review*, vol 47, pp 696-816.

Macneil, I.R. (1980) *The new social contract*, New Haven, CT: Yale University Press.

Macneil, I.R. (1985) 'Reflection on relational contract', *Zeitschrift für die gesamte Staatswissenschaft*, vol 141, pp 541-6.

Macneil, I.R. (1987) 'Barriers to the idea of relational contracts', in F. Nicklisch (ed) *The complex long-term contract*, Heidelberg: C.F. Müller Juristischer Verlad.

Macneil, I.R. (1988) 'Contractland invaded again: a comment on doctrinal writing and Shell's ethical standards', *Northwestern University Law Review*, vol 82, no 4, pp 1195-7.

Macneil, I.R. (2003) 'Reflection on relational contract theory after a neoclassical seminar', in D. Campbell, H. Collins and J. Wrightman (eds) *Implicit dimensions of contract*, Oxford: Hart Publishing, pp 207-17.

Mandag Morgen Strategisk Forum (1995) *Det sociale partnerskab (The social partnership)*, Copenhagen: Mandag Morgen.

Ministry of Social Affairs (1997) *New partnership for social cohesion*, Copenhagen: Ministry of Social Affairs.

Ministry of Social Affairs (2000a) *'Det angår os alle': Status år 2000 for kampagnen om virksomheders sociale ansvar (It regards all of us: Status year 2000 about the campaign on corporate social responsibility)*, Copenhagen: Ministry of Social Affairs.

Ministry of Social Affairs (2000b) *Det sociale indeks (The social index)*, Copenhagen: Ministry of Social Affairs.

Ministry of Social Affairs (2000c) *Samarbejdet mellem kommuner og virksomheder om arbejdsfastholdelse (The collaboration between municipalities and firms on employability)*, Copenhagen: Ministry of Social Affairs.

Moe, S. (1998) *Den moderne hjelpens sosiologi: Velferd i systemteoretisk perspektiv (The sociology of modern care: Welfare in a systems theory perspective)*, Stavanger: Apeiros Forlag.

Münch, R. (1992) 'Autopoiesis by definition', *Cardozo Law Review*, vol 13, no 5, pp 1463-71.

National Association of Local Authorities in Denmark, Ministry of Social Affairs and Ministry of Finance (2000) *Det rummelige arbejdsmarked: Kommuneaftaler juni 2000* (*The inclusive labour market: Municipal agreement June 2000*), Copenhagen.

Neu, D. (1991) 'Trust, contracting and the prospectus process', *Accounting, Organizations and Society*, vol 16, no 3, pp 243-56.

Newman, J. (2001) *Modernising governance*, London: Sage Publications.

Powell, W.W. and Smith-Doerr, L. (1994) 'Networks and economic life', in N.J. Smelsen and R. Swedberg (eds) *The handbook of economic sociology*, Princeton, NJ: Princeton University Press.

Projektrådgivningen (2006) 'Sammenslutningen af mindre NGO'er i Danmark' ('Union of small NGOs in Denmark'), pamphlet, *Projektrådgivningen*, Århus, see www.projektraadgivningen.org/downloads/projekt-net.pdf

Robert, D. (1997) 'Paradox preserved: from ontology to autology', *Thesis Eleven*, no 51, pp 53-74.

Robertson, R. (1999) 'Some-thing from no-thing: G. Spencer-Brown's laws of form', *Cybernetics and Human Knowing*, vol 6, no 4, pp 43-55.

Rummery, K. (2003) 'Progress towards partnership? The development of relations between primary care organisations and social services concerning older people's services in UK', *Social Policy and Society*, vol 3, no 1, pp 33-42.

Seal, W. (1996) 'Security design, incomplete contracts and relational contracting: implications for accounting and auditing', *British Accounting Review*, vol 28, pp 23-44.

Seal, W. (2000) *Performance indicators, regulation and management: towards responsive local governance*, Working Paper, Oslo: Norwegian School of Management, 11-14 May.

Seal, W. and Vincent-Jones, P. (1997) 'Accounting and trust in the enabling of long-term relations', *Accounting, Auditing and Accountability Journal*, vol 10, no 3, pp 406-31.

Søndergård, L. (2003) 'Offentlig-privat samarbejde på sygehuset' ('Public-private partnerships at hospitals'), in S. Hildebrandt, K.K. Klausen and S.F. Nielsen (eds) *Sygehusledelse*, Copenhagen: Munksgaard Danmark.

Spencer-Brown, G. (1969) *Laws of form*, London: George Allen and Unwin.

Stäheli, U. (2000) *Sinnzusammenbrücke: Enie dekonstruktive lektüre von Niklas Luhmanns systemteori*, Velbrück: Weilerswist.

Teubner, G. (1983) 'Substantive and reflexive elements in modern law', *Law and Society Review*, vol 17, no 2, pp 239-85.

Teubner, G. (1986) 'After legal instrumentalism?', in G. Teubner (ed) *Dilemmas of law in the welfare state*, Berlin: Walter de Gruyter.

Teubner, G. (1991) 'Autopoiesis and steering: how politics profit from the normative surplus of capital', in R. Veld, L. Schaap, C. Termeer and M. Twist (eds) *Autopoiesis and configuration theory: New approaches to social steering*, London: Kluwer Academic Publishers.

Teubner, G. (1992) 'Social order from legislative noise? Autpoietic closure as a problem for legal regulation', in G. Teubner and A. Febbrajo (eds) *State, law, and economy as autopoietic systems,* Milan: Dott. A. Giuffré Editore.

Teubner, G. (1993) 'Piercing the contractual veil? The social responsibility of contractual networks', in T. Wilhelmson (ed) *Perspectives of critical contract law*, Aldershot: Dartmouth.

Teubner, G. (1996) 'Double bind: hybrid arrangements as de-paradoxifiers', *Journal of Institutional and Theoretical Economics*, vol 152, pp 59-64.

Teubner, G. (1998) 'After privatization? The many autonomies of private law', *Current Legal Problems*, no 51, pp 393-424.

Teubner, G. (2000) 'Contracting worlds: the many autonomies of private law', *Social and Legal Studies*, vol 9, no 3, pp 399-417.

Teubner, G. (2002) 'Hybrid laws: constitutionalizing private governance networks', in R.A. Kagan, M. Krygier and K. Winston (eds) *Legality and community*, Lanham: Rowman & Littlefield Publishers.

Teubner, G. (2005) 'The anonymous matrix: human rights violations by "private" transnational actors', in M. Escamilla and M. Saavedra (eds) *Law and justice in a global society*, Granada: International Association for Philosophy of Law and Social Philosophy.

Vincent-Jones, P. (1997) 'Hybrid organization, contractual governance, and compulsory competitive tendering in provision of local authority service', in S. Deakin and J. Michie (eds) *Contract, co-operation, and competition*, Oxford: Oxford University Press.

Vincent-Jones, P. (1998) 'Responsive law in public services provision: a future for the local contracting state', *The Modern Law Review*, vol 61, no 3, pp 362-81.

Vincent-Jones, P. (1999) 'The regulation of contractualisation in quasi-markets for public services', *Public Law*, pp 303-26.

Vincent-Jones, P. (2000) 'Contractual governance: institutional and organizational analysis', *Oxford Journal of Legal Studies*, vol 20, no 3, pp 317-51.

Vincent-Jones, P. (2006) *The new public contracting*, Oxford: Oxford University Press.

Vincent-Jones, P. and Harries, A. (1995) 'Partnership and co-operation in "contracting out" local authority refuse collection services: a case study', in L. Muntanhero, R. Nunes, G. Owen and E. Rebelo (eds) *Public and private sector partnerships in the global context*, Sheffield: Pavic Publications.

Vincent-Jones, P. and Harries, A. (1996) 'Conflict and co-operation in local authority quasi-markets: the hybrid organisation of internal contracting under CCT', *Local Government Studies*, vol 22, no 4, pp 187-209.

Wiethölter, R. (1986) 'Materialization and proceduralization in modern law', in G. Teubner (ed) *Dilemmas of law in the welfare state*, New York, NY: Walter de Gruyter.

Williamson, O.E. (1975) *Markets and hierarchies: Analysis and antitrust implications*, New York, NY: Free Press.

Williamson, O.E. (1985) *The economic institutions of capitalism: Firms, markets and relational contracting*, New York, NY: Free Press.

Willke, H. (1986) 'Three types of legal structure: the conditional, the purposive and the relational program', in G. Teubner (ed) *Dilemmas of law in the welfare state*, New York, NY: Walter de Gruyter.

Willke, H. (1992a) *Ironie des Staates*, Frankfurt: Surhkamp.

Willke, H. (1992b) 'Prinzipien politischer supervision', in H. Busshoff (ed) *Politische Steurung*, Baden-Baden: Nomos Verlag, pp 51-80.

Willke, H. (1997) *Supervision des states*, Frankfurt: Surhkamp.

Wittel, A. (2001) 'Toward a network sociality', *Theory, Culture & Society*, vol 18, no 6, pp 51-76.

Index

Note: Page numbers in *italic* refer to figures and tables.